EARLY HIKING IN THE Olympics

1922 - 1942

Paul Crews

To Helga - for all of the "Mountaineers" research she selflessly performed as my old Alaskan climbing buddy!
Paul Crews
2-11-96

SEATTLE, WA
PORTLAND, OR • DENVER, CO

ISBN 0-89716-602-7
Library of Congress 95-074834
Cover and Graphic Designer: Scott Markham
Editor: Kathleen Markham

First printing
10 9 8 7 6 5 4 3 2 1

Peanut Butter Publishing
226 2nd Avenue West • Seattle, WA 98119 • (206) 281-5965
Post Office Bldg. • 510 S.W. 3rd • Portland, OR 97201 •
(503) 222-5527
Cherry Creek • 50 S. Steel • Suite 850 • Denver, CO 80209 •
(303) 322-0065
Granville Island • 1333 Johnston Street • Suite 230 •
Vancouver, BC V6H3R9 •
(604) 688-0320
e mail: PNUTPUB@aol.com

To order additional copies of this book, please contact Peanut Butter Publishing at any of the above locations.

Printed in the United States of America

TABLE OF CONTENTS

TABLE OF CONTENTS
(Continued)

ACKNOWLEDGEMENTS

Assembly of all of the events and details contained herein would have been impossible without the help and cooperation of many people, and while it is impractical to name here all of those who contributed, I am indebted to all of them.

I particularly want to thank Robert A. "Pete" Pedersen, Elvin R. "Swede" Johnson, Bob Prichard and Don R. Dooley for contributing some of the major episodes. Other surviving members of "The Club" who contributed were Alda Prichard, Viola Landry and Harry Winsor who opened up his huge store of photographs for my use, as well as his excellent memory of some of the events told here.

Contributors from various organizations include Stella Degenhardt of *The Mountaineers Historic Committee,* Jack Grauer, Historian of the *Mazamas*, Bud McCall, President of the *Klahannies* and especially Ann Moisanan, Helge Erickson and Elora Gaidrich of the *Olympians, Inc.*, who provided much documentation and stories of the Olympics in the early days. It has been a real pleasure working with them.

Dave Sicks of the *Olympic College* in Bremerton opened up his files to me, providing most of the material relating to George W. Martin. It was truly a major effort. Other contributors were Ralph Kiernan of the *Bremerton Ski Cruisers,* Ira Spring, former member of the *Shelton Ridge Runners,* Loody Cristoforo, former scout executive of the *Chief Seattle Council, BSA*, Jim Phillips, former Scout Executive of the *Tumwater Council, BSA,* Susan Schultz of the *NPS Olympic National Park Headquarters* and Billie Howard, Museum Director, *Mason County Historical Society.* Early scouting activities in the Grays Harbor area were contributed by Jim Stewart, Ed Maxey and Tony Airhart.

FOREWORD

By Dee Molenaar

This is not another of your run-of-the-mill climber's guidebooks, with all the stats covering route difficulties by Roman numerals, letters and numbers. Nor is it a treatise on the history of explorations and mountaineering in the Olympic mountains - that's already been well covered in Robert Wood's fine books. Rather, this is an enjoyable and highly personal document covering the camping, scouting, hiking and climbing activities of a bunch of relative novice climbers in the Bremerton area of Washington. Describing trips mostly during the pre-World War II era of the 1920s to 1930s and into the mid-1940s, these reminiscing accounts by Paul Crews and several of his close climbing buddies have a freshness and innocence that make for delightful bedtime reading.

Crews' first trip into the Olympics was in 1922, at age five with a family group led by his grandfather. From Bremerton in a Model-T Ford they crossed Hood Canal on the old ferry run from Seabeck to Brinnon, then drove the gravelled road around the northern perimeter, past Port Angeles and Lake Crescent to the Olympic seashore at Mora. Paul's next trip was a climb of Mt. Ellinor, his first mountain ascent, which set the stage for a lifetime love affair with the Olympic mountains.

The author briefly summarizes the early explorations into and across the mountains: north-to-south winter traverse by the Press expedition of 1889-90; the east-to-west summer crossing by the O'Neil expedition of 1890; the mapping of the Olympic Forest Preserve by Henry Gannett in 1897, and the establishment of the Olympic National Monument in 1909 and Olympic National Park in 1938. Mentioned are a few of the early pioneers Billy Everett, homesteader John Huelsdonk and wildlife photographers Herb and Lois Crisler. Details are given on the formation of the outdoors clubs that first sent hiking and climbing groups into the Olympics: *The Mazamas of Portland, The Mountaineers of Seattle, Klahhanie Club of Port Angeles, Sequim, Port Townsend and Olympians of Grays Harbor.* Also described are the author's early experiences and the leaders at several of the Boy Scout camps in the Olympics: Camp Parsons on Hood Canal, Camp Cleland on Lena Lake and Camp Baldy on Lake Quinault.

The book then covers personal accounts by Crews and his friends - Robert "Pete" Pedersen, Elvin "Swede" Johnson, Bob Prichard and Don Dooley - which cover their pioneering hikes and climbs. many of these traverse the major passes and scale adjacent peaks, with first ascents that include the spectacular Needles above Royal Basin and the spire of Mount Cruiser - named for the *Bremerton Ski Cruisers,* formed by Crews and his cronies.

I first heard of Paul Crews when as Northwest Editor for *Summit* magazine, I designed maps for a couple of articles he submitted on some of his climbs in Alaska's Chugach Range - a backdrop to his home in Anchorage. But, I first met Paul in 1960 at 14,000 feet on Mt. McKinley, where we roped together to ascend the icy slope to 16,600 feet, from where we contacted Jim and Lou Whittaker at Paul's summit camp following their accident in the John Day party higher on the peak. but, that was a bit hurried and hectic, and I saw Crews only as a bearded face behind dark goggles in a fur-lined parka - an overloaded small figure at the upper end of my rope. And, as a few of us scurried back down the mountain with the banged-up Whittakers, Paul was left behind with his Anchorage party to clean up the debris in an approaching snowstorm.

I never saw Paul again for 27 years, and then it was Elvin "Swede" Johnson, one of Paul's old Olympic climbing buddies who got Paul in on the first of our several "Old Cronies Expeditions." With George Senner we all made our first trip up Three Fingers Mountain in the Central Cascades of Washington. It was a real pleasure to finally share a climb with this near-legendary character and founder of the *Alaska Mountaineering Club*. Choosing to make his home in Anchorage following World War II, Paul is one of those rugged, self-sufficient types who has racked up enough adventures to cover several books.

PREFACE

"Absolutely breathtaking" was the comment of an acquaintance on his first visit to Seattle, "The Emerald City." He was referring to the snowcapped mountains rising to the west across Puget Sound, and I smiled, knowing that I not only concurred, but realized that he was repeating the thoughts of thousands of newcomers to the Pacific Northwest.

Nowhere, to my knowledge, can be found a group of mountains and valleys as fascinating and unique as those found on the Olympic Peninsula, the extreme northwest corner of Washington State. These are the Olympic Mountains, and they consist of over a dozen major rivers, all fanning out to all points of the compass like spokes on a wheel with their headwaters situated at or near the center of the roughly 2,500 square mile compact grouping of peaks. The ridges between rise in many places to sharp knife edges and steep pinnacles, and some of the rivers at their headwaters have active glaciers. There is an abundance of high alpine meadows, many located in picturesque high cirques of old extinct glaciers. In summer these meadows are a mass of wild flowers, of many colors, and in winter offer marvelous terrain to the more adventurous back country skier.

A feature that makes this group of mountains unique is its compactness, a mini-Switzerland. Where trails or terrain assist, a hiker may travel from any river bottom over a ridge to an adjacent river valley, or from ridge to ridge, in less than a day. A person would probably require twice as long to accomplish this in the majority of mountain ranges. These mountains are, then, a place to do a lot of hiking and see a lot of scenery in a relatively few days, and best of all be completely away from civilization.

Anyone who has seen first hand the glory of the many-colored wild flowers with deer or elk grazing nearby, the sound of the marmot's shrill voice, the spectacular view from the ridges and peaks, or the burbling of a high mountain stream next to camp, will understand this mystique. It draws a person back, again and again, and the attraction remains for life.

A number of my early climbing and hiking friends and I have kept in touch, often reminiscing over the early years, and we all feel that tales of our experiences are too important to lose. My friends and I are, therefore attempting to describe these adventures herewith.

This book, then, is about the times we had during those early days. These are presented not in the style of a historian, but rather in that of a story teller. Participants in each tale are in most cases lifetime friends, living and dead, who also have had a lifetime love of the Olympics. The stories are related on a day-to-day basis, interspersing major events with daily trivia to keep them interesting. It has been impossible for us to recall a lot of minor details, as it has been in many cases over 60 years since they occurred. All of the important, salient facts we do recall. A few of us are still living, and between us we have pieced out the details. Old photo albums and newspaper clippings, too, have been a major element in the reconstruction of these stories.

Small, unimportant details have been inserted in the stories because I used author's license to make the story more interesting and not just a dull statement of facts. I refer to such minutiae as the meals we ate. I certainly can't pinpoint what we had for any single meal, although I know we ate macaroni and cheese quite frequently and had hot oatmeal almost every breakfast. I have inserted these meals periodically.

Another item in this same category is the weather, although if we had any kind of substantial precipitation or extended clear skies it has been included, as well as swings in temperature, hot or cold.

The participants were - or are - real people, and the parts they played are authentic. Some of these friends (critics) have pointed out that I have included details in one story that actually occurred on another occasion though at the same site. My mental data bank, after 60 years, may have been zapped a time or two, but so have theirs. In any event, everything related is true to the best of our combined recollections.

I have used only material that is most outstanding in our memories. The tales I or my friends tell here we can recall quite clearly.

There are many others I could have used, but didn't as they have become too vague. Equipment, clothing and their usage are entirely different today than they were in the thirties, and this difference will be discussed herein.

The hiking population in the Olympics, too, has changed. Whereas, in earlier times a large percentage of those engaged in trekking in the Olympics had been introduced to this activity through outing groups such as *The Mountaineers* or through organized scouting activities, today this population has increased many times over. Many of the new generation of hikers are the sons and daughters or even grandchildren of the earlier adventurers. College sponsored courses and latter day outing groups have also contributed to this burgeoning generation. Unfortunately, this population explosion has in some instances overcrowded a few of the popular areas. However, do not grieve for a loss of part of the past. These overcrowded areas are few, and even though the major trails see much more travel than in the past there is still a lot of untrammeled Olympics to be found.

I have spent a week or two every August hiking or exploring in these mountains for the last eight years, continuing my Olympics adventures that had terminated in 1942. Much of this is cross-country and away from established trails. I have found that most of the locations covered herein are, in fact, just as pristine and uncrowded as they were when we earlier visited them.

There are many other places I have visited as appealing as these we have described, but I won't tell you where. You'll just have to get into the Olympics and find them for yourselves.

OLYMPIC PENINSULA

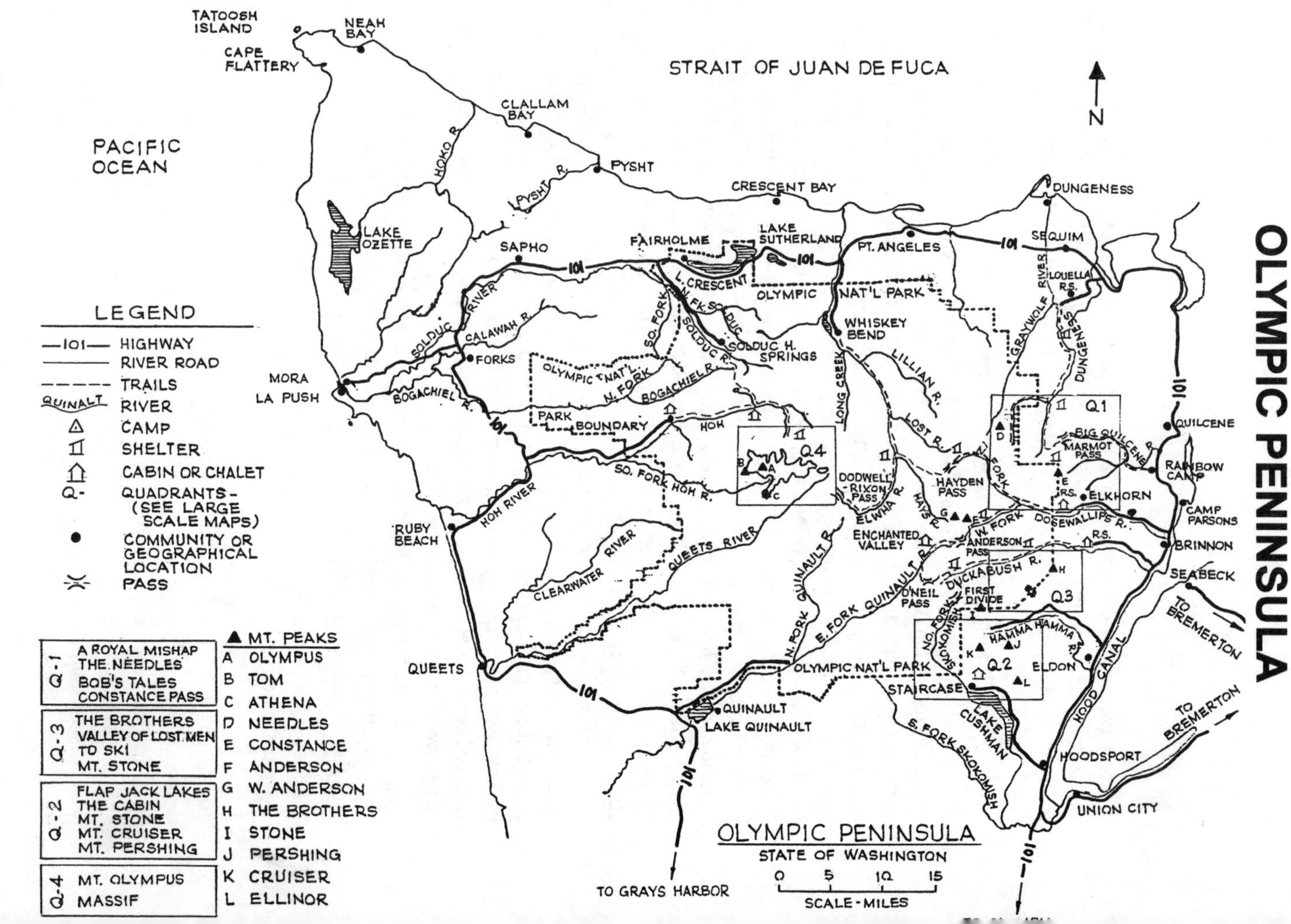

PROLOGUE

The First Years

I had my first impressions of the Olympic Peninsula in 1922 when I was five years old. Those impressions had a profound effect on my later years, as related in tales in this book. Presented herewith are three stories of that early era, which occurred less than 25 years after Lt. O'Neil's and the Press expeditions exploration parties.

Early Times

My love affair with the Olympics began at the age of five as a result of my grandfather. He came to live with us in Bremerton, Washington following the death of my grandmother. I'm sure he came west to Bremerton to rebuild his life with a complete change in his activities. The first thing he did after settling in and becoming aware of local affairs was to buy a brand new, shiny, clear isinglass-windowed top-of-the line model-T Ford touring car.

After being checked out by the local Ford agency (he had never driven before) and having received his driving license he cautiously began to explore the surrounding country, principally Kitsap County. It wasn't long before he was familiar with almost every road in the area and could do a pretty fair job of driving. At the same time he learned about fixing flat tires at the side of the road, and getting in and out of mudholes unaided. He became more and more aggressive in his exploration and kept searching for new areas to investigate.

Grandad was a well-educated man, a retired college professor who did a lot of reading, and soon became extremely interested in the Olympic Peninsula. This broadened his field of exploration, and soon he was quite familiar with Hood Canal and the narrow, twisting road that followed its southern and western shores. He studied maps, located geographical names and places, and could recite the Olympic Peninsula river names such as Skokomish, Hamma

Hamma, Duckabush, Dosewallips, Quilcene, Dungeness and Elwha likean old timer. His enthusiasm for exploration spilled over to Mom and Dad, particularly since Grandad had a car and they now had access to it.

It was June,1922, and "The Great Olympic Safari" plans were prepared. My father was working in the Puget Sound Naval Shipyard, so vacation leave was obtained and the model-T was prepared for the journey. An automobile tent was purchased. It was a three-sided shed-roofed affair, with a large flap that was secured to the top of the open fourth wall and served either as that wall, or when the car was positioned immediately adjacent to this wall the flap could be extended over the car top. This made the car the fourth wall of the tent, and access to the car's interior could be made without going outside, or a space could be left between with the flap extending to the car as a rain fly. Quite convenient. My father was very versatile with tools and made a food box about four

Camping.

feet wide, three feet high and one foot deep with little compartments anda front that dropped to become a table. This he attached to the rear bumper of the car with special brackets which he also made. When all of this had been achieved, all supplies for the expedition were loaded aboard. The gas tank and reserve gas can were filled, the departure date arrived, and we were off!

Mom and I were in the back seat, a huge pile of bedding and clothing between us and under our feet, while the large tent and some tarpaulins were tied to the running boards. The sun was rising over Manette (now East Bremerton) as we departed, for Grandad had insisted on an early start, and I was told we had a long way to travel before we camped for the night. The first leg of the journey took us north along the west side of Dyes Inlet to the small settlement of Chico, where we turned inland to the west and traveled over an "improved" county road consisting of a barely two-lane clearing with a graveled and washboardy surface. About 20 miles of this and we came to the village of Seabeck on the eastern shore of Hood Canal.

After a brief wait, the ferry that would carry us to Brinnon on the other side of Hood Canal arrived. We drove aboard, and it felt like the trip had really begun. Upon debarking in Brinnon we turned north on the Olympic Highway, following the west shore of the canal on an excellent graveled surface with very little traffic until we reached Dabob Bay where we turned inland again, away from the canal. Following the highway northwest, we climbed steadily through timbered hills until we reached the high point of the road at Rainbow Camp. This was a public camping area with a typical three-sided shake shelter. Here we had lunch and enjoyed the view of the incredible Big Quilcene River canyon that fell hundreds of feet to the narrow ribbon of river below us.

After lunch, we continued our journey north, following the two-lane highway down the side of the canyon to coastal lowlands below the towering Olympic mountains. The road took us through a mixture of logged land piled high with dead branches and fallen tree trunks, and areas of untouched timber. By late afternoon we crossed the Dungeness River, finding a place to camp for the night. A wooden irrigation flume contouring the side of a hill to the south beckoned, but my Dad, fearful of my inclination to investigate or climb anything interesting forbad my exploration. Instead I helped make camp for the night.

The first chore was to erect the tent. Previous campers had helpfully nailed a pole between two trees at exactly the right height to facilitate erecting our tent, with a fine level stretch of ground below. When the tent was acceptably pitched, Dad and Grandad started gathering wood for a fire. The firepit and a steel grating had also been left by previous campers, so the major chore was to find firewood. The surrounding wooded area had been fairly well exhausted of downed dry firewood, and it had to be located and carried from quite a distance. In the meantime, Mom and I placed a tarpaulin on the ground inside the tent and made beds for the four of us with blankets and comforters.

Mom had never cooked over an open fire before, but some of her friends in our church had given her instructions, and she had learned them well. We were served beef stew with buttered bread,cocoa and cookies. Everything was great, and rounded out an exciting day. That night we sat around the campfire and my folks discussed the trip so far, with expectations for the next day. Afterwards, Grandad also related stories about the time he had farmed in Arkansas, when he had hiked and camped there. Some of the stories about bears and wolves were pretty scary. It took me a long time to learn when Grandad was telling a story or the truth. Bedtime arrived much too early to suit me, but nevertheless I was sent to bed while my folks stayed up to enjoy the campfire a little longer. I had never slept on the ground before, and without a mattress either. The excitement of the day and new adventures I had experienced left me wide eyed. I finally dropped off to the sound of voices around the campfire and the roar of the Dungeness River.

The next morning we awakened early to another great day, and I was glad to get up. The hard ground and insufficient bedding under me left me cold long before time to rise. It didn't take the sun long to get us going again, however, and my first question was "what's for breakfast?" I soon learned. I was sent out for more firewood, and when I got back things were already under control. Breakfast consisted of hot cakes with bacon and more cocoa. I was given another chore, that of scouring the smoke-stained bottom of the frying pan with sand from the bank of the Dungeness River.

Shortly after breakfast, having repacked the model-T and cleaned up any garbage we had generated, we were on our way. We looked for a gasoline pump and found it in the small town of Dungeness, near the mouth of the Dungeness River. Fifteen miles west,along the south shores of the Straits of Juan DeFuca, we came to the logging and shipping town of Port Angeles. There was an enormous amount of logging activity in the area as shown by the bare or tangled landscape. Driving on, we came to the Elwha River which we crossed through an old fashioned covered bridge. Still on the Olympic Highway, we climbed up through a notch in a ridge and came to a beautiful lake called Sutherland. Our road passed along its northern shore, where a few small cabins could be found situated directly on the lake.

After leaving Lake Sutherland we continued through a heavily forested area until suddenly we burst out on one of the great sights on the Olympic Peninsula - Lake Crescent! We followed the Olympic Highway along its winding southern shores, impressed by the presence of Mt. Storm King looming above us. Eventually we came to the end of the lake where we entered the "Forest Reserve," and Grandad registered us before we could continue. From this point on we very seldom saw another car and entered the famous Solduc Burn area where the road cut in a straight line westward for miles and miles through nothing but tall dead scorched snags, all that remained of the former virgin forest.

That night we made camp in the rain in the little community of Rixon. In addition to the normal camp making of the night before, a tarpaulin was erected next to the fire site because of the rain, and Dad and Grandad had a very difficult time getting the fire going. With much coaxing they finally had a roaring blaze. Remembering the previous night, as well as a saturated tent floor, Dad negotiated with a farmer in the vicinity and got a load of hay to cover the floor.

I had become soaked in the rain and inevitable mud and had to change clothes, promising to stay dry and under the tarp or in the tent. The change required another cotton shirt, jacket, denim overalls, dry socks and tennis shoes. Dinner was rice and canned meat, with cocoa for me to drink and coffee for the others. It was almost as good as the previous night's meal. We still had a campfire, although it was a little difficult sitting near the fire and staying under the tarp. Bed was welcome, and I lost no time in getting to a sound sleep that lasted all night.

The road deteriorated the next day as we drove on west.

We stopped for gas at Sapho where it was still raining, but decreasing in intensity. At the end of a long, wet day we reached the end of the road at Mora. This was at the mouth of the Quilliute River, and we could see the bar across its mouth and the Pacific Ocean beyond. We camped there, our third night away from home.

Grandad wanted to go out and visit the bar and beyond, so in the morning he hired a local Indian to take us out in his open fishing boat. Dad bought a freshly caught salmon from him when we returned. After the boat trip we explored the beach and low tidal pools between

Results of a giant storm near Mora.

the mainland and a giant towering rock that became an island at high tide.

Huge waves were rolling in on the beach, so Mom, Dad and Grandad took off their shoes and stockings, stripped me down to my underwear, and we all got swished around by the surf. The water was cold, but I had never had so much fun in my life! After awhile we got dressed again, built a fire on the beach to warm up, and explored the huge piles of gigantic logs that lined the beach. Their roots were stacked up like statues, all different, and we discussed what the different ones reminded us of, everyone having a different idea.

Grandad said it was time to go, so we returned to the car and turning our backs on the Pacific Ocean reluctantly started the return drive home. Shortly after leaving Mora we came again to a giant tree that had fallen across the road, its huge root structure after it toppled being sufficient to support the trunk of the tree at least 12 feet above the highway. Automobiles continued to drive beneath the seven or eight foot diameter trunk. This was one of the thousands of forest casualties that resulted from a disastrous storm during the winter of 1921. Trees were piled up like jackstraws in all directions - a completely destroyed area.

We retraced our route of the previous days, arriving at the west end of Lake Crescent in the early evening as the sky was clearing. A beautiful camp ground for the evening was found, courtesy of the Forest Service, which had provided not only a cooking shelter complete with a steel cooking grille, but also a large stack of dry firewood. Mom cooked the salmon that Dad had obtained from the fisherman at Mora, and we all agreed it was the best fish we had ever eaten. There was a great campfire that night, and Grandad told more exciting stories, some of them true. I got to stay up until everyone went to bed, when I dropped off to sleep immediately, dreaming about Grandad's stories.

A beautiful sunrise over a dark blue Lake Crescent greeted us when we got up the next morning, and there was enough of a breeze to cause ripples on the lake's surface that sparkled like diamonds. Truly a magnificent site. Continuing on our way we contoured the south shore of Lake Crescent, then Lake Sutherland. On reaching Hood Canal we passed Brinnon, then along the south shore of Hood Canal to the pioneer community of Belfair, Union City at the head of Hood Canal, and on to Gorst on Sinclair Inlet. Very late in the evening we arrived in Bremerton and home full of experiences I had had on our journey of exploration. This all happened over 70 years ago, and although I have retraced this same route a number of times since, it still brings back many pleasant memories of my first exploration of the magnificant Olympic Peninsula.

My First Ascent

"Well, where shall we go next?" was a question put to us by Grandad shortly after our return from our exploratory camping trip to the northern Olympic Peninsula. Mom and Dad suggested that he should research the possibilities and decide, as he was the eager one. Shortly thereafter, he disclosed our destination. "We're going to climb one of those beautiful Olympic mountains. We're going to the top of Mt. Ellinor!" he stated, with overflowing enthusiasm. "There is a road to its base, and a trail to the summit!" So, in July of 1922, shortly following our return from "The Great Olympic Safari," Grandad organized our climbing expedition.

It was decided that the party would consist of we four and another family, the Criders. The members of the Crider family were our close friends: George, Ione, and their daughter Helen who was three years older than I. Both families had Model-T's and were equally equipped for camping, so it was just a matter of setting a date and going. When all of this was accomplished, we headed for the Olympics.

Our route took us along the south shore of Hood Canal until we reached the community of Hoodsport, where we turned west away from Hood Canal and continued inland, more or less following a narrow one-and-a half lane road until we came to Lake Cushman. As we approached the lake, we noticed that a large area around the lake had been extensively logged and all debris from the operation removed. This had been done because the City of Tacoma intended to raise the level of the lake with a new dam and provide hydroelectric power for that city.

Our first view of the Lake was provided as the small narrow

The Cushman House.

lane road took us along the top of one of the hills surrounding the lake. The view from here was breathtaking, disclosing the ultimate extent of the flooding as delineated by the newly-logged land. Below us we could see the guest hotel "The Antlers" and farther along the lake another hotel, the "Cushman House", early commercial enterprises of the area. Both of these would be under a hundred feet of water within the next several years. Through groves of fir and maple we forded a branch of the Skokomish River and selected a campsite on the banks of Lake Cushman. That night there was a big campfire. The discussion was primarily about the next two days' climb and what we could expect. It was a new experience for all.

The next morning we arose quite early, and Dad, George and Grandad started putting together the packs that would carry what we would need for the first night out. These packs consisted of typical prospector packboards, carryovers from the Alaskan gold rush.

When everything was ready we started for the mountain. Dad, George and Grandad were the load bearers while Mom, Ione, Helen and I each carried a change of clothes, toothbrush, etc., in little packsacks. The trail crossed Big Creek, then passed through deep meadows of grass until it reached the site of an abandoned large two-story house in perfect condition. This was the private home of the A.G.Cushman Family, soon to be inundated by the new Lake.

The trail broke from the meadow and started switchbacking up a steep ridge. On the right we could hear the rush of a mountain stream and discovered that there was a small dam and a Pelton Wheel that had been the source of electric energy for the Cushmans. Our trail continued on up a ridge, and after about four hours of climbing (and resting) we passed a waterfall on our right. The men decided that because we were near water, there was a flat spot on which to camp, and because they estimated we were over halfway up (and all tired) we should camp for the night.

The Criders had brought a small lightweight oiled silk tent that was barely adequate to accommodate the entire family. The rest of us had no tent, but my father had brought a canvas tarp large enough to give us cover in case of rain, so we were set for the night. There was another campfire, but it didn't last long as everyone was ready for bed.

In the morning we were eager to be on our way. The trail took a turn to the right at this point, passing above the falls and crossing through rockslides and slopes dotted with a profusion of wild flowers - Indian paintbrush, lilies, daisies and many other - then through dense stunted alpine firs where moss covered everything and hung in streamers from every leaning tree.

"That Little Lake" from the summit of Mt. Ellinor.

Grandad, who was leading, suddenly stopped and held up his hand for silence. Then he slowly pointed ahead, and there we saw a grouse in the trail. We approached slowly, but it suddenly flew off a few feet, then stopped to watch. Upon approaching closer, the same thing occurred. Grandad stopped again, beckoned us to come closer, and pointed to a number of tiny grouse chicks clustered together. Their mother obviously had been trying to lure us away from her little ones by making her short flights. Being careful not to disturb them, we passed by and continued up the trail. A short time later Grandad again held up his hand, and we all stopped, this time in anticipation of what he had found. It was a small rabbit that wasted no time in hopping away out of sight.

We came to a fork in the trail just beyond there, and after much discussion, it was decided to take the right branch which appeared the more heavily traveled. This led for a short distance, then crossed a steep slope covered with a large field of snow (the first snow we had seen all day). It was decided for safety reasons we could go no further on this trail. It was also at about this time that Dad and Mom proceeded to install a dog leash on me, to keep me, as Mom said, "from darting around off the trail, up rocks, chasing birds, and acting like a puppy dog." I was quite incensed at this, asking why Helen didn't have to wear a leash. Mom's comment was "Helen is acting like a little lady." My only thought was that I was glad I wasn't acting like a little lady.

Having retraced our steps to the fork in the trail, we took the left branch this time and climbed through the most beautiful display of wildflowers you could imagine. We were getting really high now, basically above timberline, and I was entranced. This was my kind of country. I wanted to go on and on through these great meadows. I just couldn't get enough of them. Suddenly as we came around the corner of a rocky ridge we startled a feeding deer, and she bounded away in great leaps, vanishing from view around another rock outcropping. Boy, it was beginning to be the most exciting day of my life!

We continued through more meadows, still climbing, and found ourselves approaching the saddle that separates Mt. Ellinor and Mt. Washington. It was at this point that Dad raised his hand for silence, then pointed, and I saw about three feet of tawny tail disappear behind a rock. Dad insisted that he had seen a real live cougar, and I insisted with him that I had seen three feet of cougar tail. I really had something to tell the kids back home - I had seen a real live cougar's tail!

We had only reached the saddle, but I saw the top of Mt. Ellinor beckoning me. It was irresistable, and I had to get there. The only thing holding me back was that darned dog leash. I practically dragged Dad to the top of the peak. I had never seen ranges of mountains stacked up peak beyond peak beyond peak before, many of them capped with snow. I was fascinated, wanting nothing more than to sit there and look. Ultimately this had to end, my empty stomach calling me back to the saddle where everyone was having lunch.

After lunch we did a little exploring, and the worst experience of the day happened! I looked over the north edge of the saddle and saw nothing below me for several hundred feet, with a little lake at the very

Me, Mom, Dad and Grandad on the top of Mt. Ellinor.

bottom! I was terrified. What if I had gone charging over there without the dog leash! I pulled back and stayed as far away from it as I could, and was ready to leave for home.

The return was uneventful - no more deer, rabbits or grouse. My experience at the saddle had also dampened my enthusiasm for the flower-filled slopes. We were suddenly startled at one point by a loud, piercing whistle. Grandad said it must be one of those marmots he had read about, although we never did see it.

We reached our last night's campsite, packed up and started down the mountain at a much greater rate than when we had climbed it the day before. Upon reaching the cars everybody had a sort of picnic with whatever food was left over, and wonder of wonders I had recovered from the earlier cliff episode. Once again my thoughts were on those marvelous many-colored meadows and I wondered if I would see a whole cougar on our next trip.

After saying goodby to the abandoned A.G. Cushman home before inundation, we drove on home to end an unforgettable trip, and the ascent of my first mountain.

Up and Down "The Dose"

"I can hardly wait until summer," was Grandad's major theme

of conversation all winter, and we knew he definitely wanted to continue his exploration of the Olympic Peninsula. His desires were satisfied when the Criders suggested that we make another camping trip, this time to the Dosewallips River where the Criders had been before and had described its wonders in glowing terms. It didn't take much conversation for the decision to be made. It would be a camping trip that included lots of fishing and hiking.

George Crider was a very experienced fisherman and had caught all of the rainbow trout they could eat last time. Now with more mouths to feed he could with a clear conscience go for even more fish. Dad and Grandad weren't into fishing much, but were intrigued by the great hiking prospects presented and were willing to try a little fishing, too. Apparently Mom, Ione and Helen were content to hike, enjoy nature, and in Mom's case do little charcoal sketches of what she saw and liked. As for me, it all sounded wonderful and I wanted to do everything suggested.

This time the expedition was scheduled for July, 1923 and would cover a greater period of time, so more complicated preparations were in order. We would be backpacking up the "Dose" for two days plus several days at a base camp, as well as the hike out. Everybody had to carry their share of the supplies. The men would have their large packboards, and the rest of us would pack knapsacks of personal clothing, toilet articles and a portion of the food. The men's load, which included the bulk of the food and all of the bedding must have been very heavy.

George took Dad, Grandad and me shopping for fishing gear and advised us on what to purchase. He was an avid fly fisherman, so the men got fly rods, flies, line, etc., and when I asked about my fishing tackle I was informed that George knew just the right kind of bush where we were going that would provide an excellent pole for me. There were no fly rods on sale that were my size. I accepted their word for it, and didn't regret it as later events showed.

Departure day arrived, and we were away in the two Model-T's, driving around Hood Canal. Several miles north of Brinnon we crossed the Dosewallips River and turned left off the Olympic Highway onto a little single lane dirt road that followed inland beside the Dosewallips. We had not traveled very far when we saw a sign that read

"Rockybrook Falls" with an arrow pointing up a small stream to our right. Grandad insisted that we stop and investigate, so we got out and hiked up the trace of a trail toward the ever increasing sound of roaring water. I had never seen so much water falling in one place in my life. Of course, after all the new and fascinating sights I had seen last year I was beginning to take these things in stride. After all, how could this compare with that gigantic cliff I had seen on Mt. Ellinor last year? After while, Dad said he had taken all the pictures he thought we could use so we drove on.

About a mile of traveling through meadows near the river bank brought us to the end of the road and Corregenda Ranger Sttion. The cars were parked off the road, the isinglass-sided curtains installed to protect the interior from rain, packs shouldered, and we were off on our great river exploration.

The road followed fairly close to the river, through cleared land with occasional small patches of maple and fir or spruce. The roar of the river was always with us, and we would occasionally stop to pick salmonberries from the heavily loaded vines. Lunch time arrived, and we stopped in a cleared meadow with an unoccupied house and lean-to near the river. A crude sign announced that this was "the Archer Place." It was apparent that Mr. Archer was not home.

After a lunch of sandwiches brought from home we travelled several miles more and came to "Mountain Home," a log cabin located on a hill above the river, with a shake shelter nearby. We speculated that Mr. Archer had used it as a trapper's cabin.

The decision was made to camp there where previous campers had made some improvements to facilities, and the lean-to was clean and dry for sleeping. George immediately got out his fishing gear and attacked "Dose" with a vengeance, with the result that we all had trout for dinner - as much as we could eat and enough left over for breakfast.

The weather had been overcast when we left Bremerton, but when we woke up in the morning we really had a new day. The sun was just coming up over the hills to the east with not a cloud to be seen, and the trail was waiting. After fried trout and pancakes everyone packed up, and we were off. The terrain had changed from open meadows to heavy timber beyond the Archer Place. The warming sun had a hard time penetrating the forest to reach us, but what with packs and hard work no one seemed to be cold.

Mountain Home camp.

At noon we reached Elkhorn Camp where we had lunch of more cold sandwiches from home, then continued on up the river to a small log cabin and a Forest Service shelter. A sign over the door indicated that this was the Jump-off Ranger Station and sure enough, there was a ranger and his wife who welcomed us to the Upper Jump-off. They suggested that we occupy the shelter, as it was there for hikers such as us and best of all had a large supply of dry wood, courtesy of the Forest Service.

Mom and Ione went to work making the shelter into our new home for the next several days while Helen and I explored the country beyond the cabin, having received instructions to stay within sight. Helen was very careful to follow these instructions and wouldn't let me be a little more exploratory, so everyone was happy, but me.

George got out the fishing gear and took Dad and Grandad down to the river where a course in fly fishing got under way, and although George was the big winner the other two didn't do too badly. We had trout again for dinner, and Dad said that since he had caught the ones he was eating they were the best he had ever had.

Camp Muscott (Jump-Off Ranger Station).

After dinner George took me to the river and, cutting me a fishpole from a willow bush, he showed me how to tie some *cuttihunk* fish line on to the pole and tie a fly on the other end of the line. Then the lesson began, and I discovered that if I would put the fly upstream and let it drift down with the current I could occasionally catch a fish. I caught a couple that George said would make a good breakfast for me. Then we went up to the shelter and listened to Grandad tell more of his tales. I had heard some of them before, but Helen had not and she was really fascinated. When I advised her later that a lot of them he had just made up, she really was upset. She thought I was terrible for suggesting that he had told a fib.

The next morning Dad, Grandad and George packed up again, planning to leave us for three days while they hiked on up to Hayden Pass at the headwaters of the Dosewallips, the divide between the "Dose" and the Elwha River. I pleaded and pleaded for them to take me, too, but to no avail. Shortly after they left it began to cloud over, and Mom and Ione were concerned that the men would get rained out. When I thought about this I was almost glad that I didn't get to go with them although the memories of those alpine meadows I had experienced the previous year still were attracting me.

I suddenly remembered the fish I had caught the night before and had eaten for breakfast, and I prepared to go fishing. Just as I was dropping down to the river and last night's fishing hole, Mom shouted to me to come back. I was informed that I could not go down to the river unless there was an adult with me, I assume for the same reasons as the "puppy dog" scolding I had received last year on Mt. Ellinor. All of a sudden Helen spoke up in my defense, stating that she would keep an eye on me if I started to stray from the "safe" beach where I had fished with George. As Helen was only three years older than I, it didn't seem reasonable that her judgement was any better than mine, but under the circumstances I couldn't complain. Then I remembered that "Helen was a little lady" and had set me free to go fishing.

I caught one fish in about half an hour, and was still casting like George taught me when something grabbed my line and broke off the only fly that I had. That seemed to have ended my fishing until George got back. The ranger, who was getting ready to hike up the trail for some chore or other, came to my rescue. He told me that he had no flies, but something that was just as good. He went into the cabin and returned with half a dozen plain barbed fish hooks and showed me how to tie them on the line. Then we went out in the adjacent brush and in five minutes had a dozen little black beetles that he showed me how to attach to the hook. I said goodbye with many thanks as he started up the trail, and Helen and I headed for the river.

The beetles worked better than the fly. Helen got excited and we rigged up a pole, line and hook for her, too. From then on, we were real buddies, improving our fishing skills together. Helen may have been a "little lady," but she sure was not squeemish about taking fish off and putting bugs on the hook.

The next day Mom, Ione, Helen and I took an all-day hike up the trail toward Hayden Pass. After several miles we came to the Forks Camp where we stopped for lunch. This camp was at the juncture of the Dosewallips and West Fork Dosewallips. While we were trying to decide which branch we should explore, it started to rain and a decision was made. We headed for Upper Jump-off as fast as we could go. We were pretty wet when we got there as we had not taken rain coats, so we spent the afternoon drying out our wet clothes. I changed into my spares which consisted of cotton shirt, blue overalls, dry socks and tennis shoes. My Li'l Abner boots were soaked. That night we went to bed in the shelter to the combined sound of rain on the shed roof and the roar of the river.

It was still raining the next morning,. Because of the rain, Mom and Ione were quite concerned about the status of the men who were up the trail. However, shortly before dark the next day the missing men arrived in camp, soaking wet and ravenous. The women had anticipated this and had a huge stew with bread and butter and coffee for them in short order. First, however, they changed from their soggy clothes and hung them around the leanto on every hook, nail, and clothes line they could find. At least ours were dry by then and out of the way. The odor of drying wool was pretty strong, but didn't deter them from enjoying their meal as they cleaned the pot.

After dinner we stoked up the fire to help dry out the curtain of clothes suspended around the fire and waited to hear about the trip the men had just completed. Grandad was elected their spokesman, and with many interruptions from Dad and George, he related their experiences. Under lowering skies they had proceeded on up the trail until late in the day they had arrived at Bear Camp just as it began to rain. Not having a tent, they started building a lean-to from fir branches

Bear Camp (note lean-to on left).

just as the ranger arrived from below.

He offered some advice on the lean-to's construction, then went on up the trail to the Dose Meadows shelter where he was going to spend the night. Having completed the shelter, they set about getting a fire going for dinner with much difficulty because of the wet firewood, and finally succeeded after using upmost of their available toilet paper as tinder.

Disaster struck shortly, for someone had kicked over the coffee pot, spilling it on the fire and almost putting it out. It was not a good beginning for an evening that got worse. The lean-to leaked, and because of the rain and higher elevation they experienced a very cold night. Fortunately they kept the fire going and were able to have a good breakfast although it was still raining a little.

Leaving their packs in the lean-to they started on up the trail toward Hayden Pass in a rain that never stopped. They missed the Dose Meadows shelter, as it was off the main trail and concealed in a grove of spruce trees. At this point the rain became mixed with snow. Residual snow drifts became more frequent and larger. They finally reached the pass and although they could look to the west down the Hayes River Valley, a tributary of the Elwha River, it was choked with clouds, and visibility was nil. This condition was pretty much the same in the Dosewallips Valley, as well, and they decided to return to camp.

Dad had exposed the entire roll of film in his camera so they took timeout to change film in a snow cave under a large snowbank formed by the flowing Dosewallips. Their feet were wet, their raincoats leaked, and they had had enough of Dose Meadows for that day. Upon reaching Bear Camp they picked up their packs and headed down the valley to a better campsite at a lower, warmer elevation.

Camp was made at a fairly large stream from the north (probably Deception Creek), and they prepared a much better lean-to than at Bear Camp. The fire start was still a problem, but they had learned from Bear Camp and had carried a small supply of dry wood from there. In the morning they got an early start down the river. Their thoughts wereon something dry at the Upper Jump-0ff. The trip back was uneventful, and they reached us late that afternoon.

The next morning everyone slept in but Helen and me. We went fishing and had enough for breakfast for everyone. George was quite surprised, thinking we had done it with his deceased fly. Helen couldn't let that pass, however, and explained how we were so successful. He didn't say anything, but I think there was a look of disapproval on his face.

The weather had cleared during the night and the sun was warm and bright. We stayed in camp until just before noon, drying the last of the men's clothes, and then packed up. After saying goodbye to the ranger and his wife, we started down the trail with "Mountain Home" as our next camp. The great weather and the thought of more fishing that night made it a short trip for me, and I could hardly wait to get George down at the river to watch me catch fish. George, Helen and I went fishing as soon as we arrived, and Helen and I were catching more fish than George which he took with good grace. He taught me something on that trip, though. Everyone had had enough trout diet for the entire week, so George showed us how to carefully unhook each fish and return it to the river.

We still had our fabulous weather the next day and made short work of hiking on out to Correganda Ranger Station and the cars. As could be predicted, the return trip to Bremerton was uneventful. It was too bad that the weather had been great when we started the trip, lasted for two days, turned sour for the three days the men had hiked up to what I considered the best country, then turned fine again after their return to base camp.

I was anxious to get into the high alpine meadow country again, and hoped that next time I would get to Dose Meadows and all those beautiful mountain flowers. Their attraction, since my first introduction to them on Mt. Ellinor, has always remained with me and has had a major influence on my life.

CHAPTER 1 OUTDOOR ORGANIZATIONS

Access to the wonders of the Olympic mountains' high meadows, glaciers and wildlife was not always as easy to attain as it is today. The early development of recreational activities in the Olympics, primarily hunting, fishing, hiking, climbing and photography, is described herein, but first a little bit of history should be included to bring into perspective the size and basically natural state of the Olympic mountains. The perimeter of the central portion has been almost totally stripped of first growth timber, but in many areas has partially recovered because of the maturing of second growth trees. The central core, however, has been untouched and will hopefully remain so, as it is now a part of the protected Olympic National Park. Furthermore, many of the sections outside of the park and under control of the National Forest Service have been designated Wilderness Areas and are also protected. How this came about is described hereafter.

The Olympics would not be as clean and unspoiled as they are today if it had not been for the efforts of many individuals and organizations who started early on to protect the great assets of the entire Olympic Peninsula. A short summary of the history of early exploration and these efforts follows:

The original major exploration of the Olympic mountains interior, first by an army expedition led by Lt. Joseph P. O'Neil, was carried out in 1885 in the northern part of the mountains, primarily south of Port Angeles. Lt. O'Neil's intent to explore a larger area was called off because of orders transferring him to another duty station.

Five years later his initial efforts were followed by the Press expedition during the winter of 1889-90, a civilian venture sponsored by a newspaper, the *Seattle Press*. The party chose to make the trip during the winter, and although successful nearly perished from starvation and cold. They traversed the Olympics from north to south, traveling up the Elwha river and Goldie Creek, over the Low Divide and down the North Fork of the Quinault River.

Lt. O'Neil once again led an expedition to the Olympics during the summer of 1890, sponsored jointly by the Army and the Oregon Alpine Club, with civilian scientists from that club participating. This time Lt. O'Neil's party traversed the Olympics interior from east to west, traveling up the North Fork Skokomish river, through the Lake LaCrosse basin, then exiting in two parties.

One party crossed the Burke Range to the Elwha Basin, traveled over the soon-to-be-named Dodwell-Rixon Pass and down the Queets River To tidewater, and some of the party is believed to have climbed the South Peak of Mt. Olympus en route. The other party traveled down the East Fork of the Quinault River.

It was in 1897 that Washington D.C. dispatched Henry Gannet, Chief Geographer of the U.S. Geological Survey, to the Olympic Peninsula to survey the range in preparation for the establishment of the Olympic Forest Reserve. He was fortunate in securing the help of Arthur Dodwell and Theodore Rixon, who with four assistants surveyed over 3,400 square miles in the years 1898,1899 and 1900.

These expeditions basically opened up the mountains to individual travel, primarily from newly established trails over their routes, as well as maps the explorers had prepared, including names of natural features. The natural beauty and state of wilderness in its present condition, however, can be attributed to early action by many individuals and organizations dedicated to protecting what was then known as "The Last Frontier."

In chronological order, follow the salient events that have led to the current Olympic National Park status:

1. Judge James Wickersham, while on a private family expedition into the heart of the Olympic mountains met Lt. O'Neil on his 1890 expedition and was impressed by what he heard and saw. He wrote two letters dated November 3 and 8, 1890 to Washington, D.C. describing the beauty and outstanding flora and fauna, with suggestions and arguments for the formation of a national park.

2. The Act of 1891 was enacted, setting aside 13,000,000 acres

nationally in Forest Reserves under the control of the Department of the Interior.

3. In 1897 a preserve of about 2,200,000 acres was created and called the Olympic Forest Preserve.

4. This preserve was reduced by about 712,000 acres in 1900 and 1901 under pressure from the timber industry.

5. It was not this timber deletion that sparked efforts to protect the area as Judge Wickersham had suggested, however, but protection of the wildlife - namely the great elk herds that were being depleted by hunters. As a result of the elk problem President Theodore Roosevelt in 1909 signed an executive order creating the 611,000 acre Mount Olympus National Monument. Shortly thereafter the elk herds became known as "Roosevelt Elk" and are thus named today.

6. After World War I, the acreage of the monument was dropped by about half by order of President Wilson. That signalled ever increasing bickering between logging and mining interests on one hand, and conservation groups on the other.

7. President Franklin D. Roosevelt in 1933 transferred all National monuments that were in National Forests to the National Park Service.

8. In 1938, President Roosevelt signed the bill creating the Olympic National Park, encompassing 638,280 acres.

While a few individuals, such as Judge Wickersham, were exploring early trails, and pioneer residents of the Olympic Peninsula Billy Everett and John Huelsdonk were hunting, trapping and developing new trails into the interior prior to World War I, there was very little other activity. In the years following World War I, Herb Crisler, a wildlife photographer, and his wife Lois did much to publicize the beauty of the Olympic mountains, most of their activities remote from established roads and trails.

Between about 1900 and 1920 a number of hiking and mountaineering clubs made annual outings to the Olympics, among them *The Mazamas, The Mountaineers, the Klahhanes* and later the *Grays Harbor Olympians*. These were primarily only once-a-year events in those days; however, with only a few dozen participants per club. There were undoubtedly many individual efforts by club members on their own. These clubs, and their goals are listed herewith.

THE MAZAMAS

The Mazamas really knew how to throw a party! The first organizational meeting was scheduled for July 19, 1894 on the summit of Mt. Hood, with speeches, a festive banquet and fireworks to proclaim to the world that the Mazamas were born!

A total of about 250 people started up the mountain on the great day from Camp Mazama, the first leaving at three in the morning. They arrived at the meeting place on top a little after 8:00 a.m., and later arrivals were all at the summit by 2:30 p.m. Unfortunately, there were high winds with blowing snow on the upper mountain, and the party never came off as planned. The earlier climbers left almost immediately, and as they passed those still climbing strongly suggested that they abandon their efforts and retreat to the safety of Camp Mazama. As a result many turned around and followed the others down.

A second group of about 50 people started up the mountain from Cloud Camp, on the opposite side of the mountain from Government Camp, and approximately 25 reached the summit. A hardy group of club officers, charged with the duty of an organizational meeting, quickly conducted their business in a cold, whistling wind before hurrying off the summit. Of the approximately 300 starters, 155 men and 35 women actually reached the peak although only about 40 remained for the organizational meeting.

The meeting was called to order by temporary chairman Rev. Earl M. Wilbur and the following officers were elected:

President: William G. Steel
Vice-President: Rev. Wilbur
H.D.Langille
C.H.Chapman
A.H.Johnson
Secretary: E.H.Sholes

Treasurer: Francis C. Little
Historian: Fay Fuller
Exec.Cncl: Ida McElvain
Della Watson
E.C.Stuart

The meeting was hastily adjourned and the officers retired to a more hospitable environment.

Although fireworks were on the schedule for the evening of the 19th, only a few in the neighboring lowland towns thought they had seen the display because of cloud cover.

Membership requirements for the Mazamas consisted of the candidate's having successfully climbed on foot a mountain having an active glacier on its slopes. Mt. Hood qualified for the mountain. Of the 193 summiters on July 19, 1894, 105 applied for membership and thus, became charter members. Other successful climbers applied later.

The Mazamas became a mountaineering club only a year or two after the formation of the *Sierra Club* and many of the members had previously belonged to the defunct *Oregon Alpine Club*. A number of the members had previously been members of both these earlier clubs.

Will Steel was an ideal first president, as he had strong feelings about appreciation of the mountains. He was a conservationist and successfully pursued a personal goal of promoting Crater Lake to the status of a National Park. He was able to keep the membership well informed about club activities with the publication of his mountaineering journal *Steel Points*.

All of the early annual outings of the Mazamas were held in the Cascades, and the Olympic mountains were virtually untouched until 1928, although there were certainly a few individual members who explored the Olympics earlier. Nineteen-twenty-eight was the year when the outing committee scheduled a climb of Mt. Olympus. The entire trip lasted about two weeks, beginning July 29,1928, with 60 members participating.

The route followed the North Fork Quinault River and over the Low Divide to the base camp in the Elwha Basin. Intermediate camps were at nine-mile and Low Divide, with a side trip to the summit of Mt. Christie.

From Elwha Basin an advance camp was located in the Queets Basin, and on August 5th a party of 33 started up the Humes Glacier, passed through Blizzard Pass, up the Hoh Glacier until just south of Olympus' Middle Peak, which they all managed to climb. Four of the group continued on to also climb the West Peak. Visibility was poor, and but for that, all 33 might have made the West Peak, too.

Return to the Queets Basin was made that same day, and on August 6th the entire party returned to the base camp in the Elwha Basin. Members climbed other peaks adjacent to the Basin including Teter Top and Mt. Meany, and on August 9th started the return to the Quinault trailhead.

Since that first outing in 1928 the Mazamas have made a number of subsequent climbs in the Olympics.

THE MOUNTAINEERS

Another of the mountain clubs, The Mountaineers, was formed in 1906, originally as an auxiliary of the Mazamas, but in 1907 dropped the auxiliary affiliation and became officially called "The Mountaineers." Professor Henry Landes, Dean of Geology at the University of Washington was the first president in 1907, followed in 1908 by Professor Edmond S. Meany, also of the University of Washington who led the club for 28 consecutive years until 1935, his popularity evidence of his leadership and ability to help The Mountaineers mature.

The Mountaineers' activities were quite broad, and their hiking and climbing parties participated from the beginning in trips all over the Northwest - The Olympics, Cascades, the great volcanic peaks Hood, Adams, Glacier Peak, St. Helens and Baker, but most of all Mt. Rainier. A study of Mt. Rainier's exploratory days is full of references to activities of The Mountaineers and geographic locations named by them. Professor Meany in his book *Mt. Rainier, A Record of Exploration,* presents much of these activities.

But our interest herein is primarily about hiking and climbing in the Olympic Mountains. The Mountaineers made large group expeditions seven times until the present day, as follows:

1907: 65 members made a three-week penetration of the Olympics, and in addition to the first ascent of the West Peak of Mt. Olympus, also scaled the other "6,000+" peaks at the Olympics core: Olympus Middle Peak, East Peak, Mts. Meany, Barnes, Queets, Seattle,

Noyes and Christie.

1913: 106 members, with pack horses, traversed the Olympics from north to south from Port.. Angeles to Tahola, following the tracks of the 1889-1890 Press expedition.

1920, 1926, 1933, 1940 and 1951: Additional outings similar to those listed above.

KLAHHANE CLUB

The Klahhane Club originated on March 4, 1915 in Port Angeles. It was started by a dozen or so members at the home of Mr. and Mrs. Ben Phillips. Ben Phillips, founder of the local banking interests, became the first president.

"Klahhane," I am told, means "good times out of doors" and this has remained the club's goal. Hiking, camping, picnicking, and traveling together are just part of the club's activities. Originally, the club considered becoming part of The Mountaineers, but later decided to remain separate. Old records mention The Mountaineers frequently, so apparently the ties were great.

The club had various club houses until the early 1930's when the present one at Lake Dawn was built by the members. It is built of logs and hand-split shakes, complete with a rock fireplace.

Originally the club house was open to the public and featured a beautiful garden, which was developed by E.B. Webster, a club member and newspaper publisher in Port Angeles. The interior was a museum containing many exhibits. Recently, after several items were stolen, all of the artifacts were donated to the Clallam County Museum.

The club had always promoted conservation and worked hard on the movement to establish the Olympic National Park. Its efforts were successful, and the park became a reality in 1938.

Trail work parties are still held a few times each year, and day hikes are held two or three times each week, year around. In addition, car camps and backpacking trips are held in the summer.
Large groups on the trail are discouraged, and their number restricted.

Club membership is made up of members from Port Angeles,

Sequim and Port Townsend. There is a close relationship with the *Victoria Outing Club*, and visitations are held between the two clubs.

THE OLYMPIANS

In 1920 the Grays Harbor area, primarily the twin cities of Aberdeen and Hoquiam, was a bustling center for the timber, shipping and fishing industries for the southwest section of the State of Washington.

Mr. Frank H. Lamb, a community leader in the area, had spent much of his free time hiking the Olympic mountain trails, and on one of his trips met with and was a guest of The Mountaineers when they were on their 1920 extended trip into the Olympics. He was very much impressed with their activities, and sensing a need for a similar organization in Grays Harbor, he contacted people in the area with like interests. And so was born "The Olympians."

Another hiking enthusiast, one of the persons contacted by Frank Lamb, was Oscar C. Lovgren who contributed a wealth of experience to the organization. His entire adult life was devoted to the youth of the area, primarily through the local YMCA. He was there from 1910 until 1950, when he retired. The last thirty-six years of this period was as general secretary.

During most of his career he spent his summers operating YMCA outdoor youth camps and leading hiking groups for extended periods throughout the Olympics. By 1920, when the Olympians were born, he already had the leadership experience to be a major promoter of Olympian hiking jaunts. He probably brought along many new Olympians members with him, former "Oscar's Boys".

In addition to his full time YMCA work, he also devoted time to the Girl Scout organization in the Grays Harbor area. It was no surprise, then, that he and Frank H. Lamb formed a marvelous team in guiding the Olympians in their formative years. The first preliminary Olympian meeting was held on September 29, 1920, presided over by Mr. Frank H. Lamb as temporary chairman. The Olympians became "official" on October 27, 1920 when the constitution was adopted, and Frank H. Lamb became the first president. All those present at this second meeting became charter members, as follows:

Frank H. Lamb	W.L.Cuthbertson
Howard Oakland	O.C. Lovgren
Agnes V. Johnson	John Somerville
Isla Roisom	K.C. Berg
Mrs. Harvey Lord	L.M. Cooper
Alison Emerson Lamb	Charles Albertson

The club's first officers were:

President: Frank H. Lamb	Directors:
Vice President: O.C. Lovgren	Mrs. Walter Slade
Secretary: Agnes V. Johnson	K.C. Berg
Treasurer: Howard Oakland	Hugo Nelson

The early Past Presidents were:

1920-21 Frank H. Lamb	1926-27 Frank H. Lamb
1921-22 O.C. Lovgren	1927-28 Frank H. Lamb
1922-23 Frank H. Lamb	1928-29 F.W. Mathias
1923-25 (info. missing)	1929-30 Blanch Fulton
1925-26 Frank H. Lamb	1930-31 Tony Forest

Frank H. Lamb was elected President Emeritus in 1929.

The Olympians incorporated in 1935, to become THE OLYMPIANS, INC. Since then, the Olympians have made three extended two-week hikes into the Olympics, utilizing pack horses to eliminate some of the less desirable elements of backpacking. These hikes were:

1921 Mt. Olympus via Low Divide & Dodwell-Rixon Pass
1926 Mt. Olympus via Elwha Basin & Humes Glacier
1934 Mt. Olympus via Glacier Meadows

In other years there have been numerous backpacking hikes of shorter duration - two or three a year, as well as hikes and climbs in the Cascades including the volcanic peaks.

One three-year project of which the Olympians are quite proud was the complete renovation of the Enchanted Valley Chalet, originally built in 1930. In 1938 when the East Fork Quinault River valley was incorporated into the Olympic National Park, the Park Service took over ownership of the Chalet, previously constructed and operated by the Olympic Recreation Co. as a commercial hotel. The new owners were not inn keepers and by 1980 the facility was in need of major repairs. The Olympians asked permission of the Park Service to make the necessary repairs which was finally granted. Thousands of man-hours of labor and helicopter time over three summers - 1983, 1984 and 1985 - were required to completely renovate the Chalet, including air lifting replacement logs for the rotting foundations, installation of new floors and windows and complete reconstruction of the chimney.

The Olympians are now preparing for the 75th Anniversary of the club's formation. May it be one of many happy anniversaries for them!

President Lamb, in his later years, wrote several articles about hiking and climbing in the Olympics, and the following quotation tells it all:

"I have made many trips into the Olympics, but more than 20 years ago, I found it necessary to forego the more strenuous tramping and climbing efforts. Since then, I have had to be content with such high points as I could reach on horseback, by auto or by air. Besides visiting every mountain region in North America, I have threaded the splendid highways and traveled the cog railroads of Switzerland, motored down the alpine valleys to the fjords of Norway, ascended high on the precipitous flanks of Aorangi, 'the cloud-piercer' of New Zealand's Southern Alps and looked down upon the Andes from the air. They are all grand and inspiring, but there is no pleasure that can compare with those days of youth with pack on back, high on an Olympic trail."

CHAPTER 2
BACKPACKING

The horse and buggy days are behind us, thankfully, and so are the outdoor hiking and camping equipment and methods described for nearly all of the episodes related hereafter, covering the period from about 1925 to 1945. Those were the good old days, and the reader will be able, at the end of this chapter, to compare equipment and methods used then and now. Hiking treks into the Olympic Mountains were nearly all planned to coincide with good weather. The Forest Service had very kindly, in addition to providing excellent trails, also erected shelters about every five or ten miles, negating the necessity for tents. The optimum time of year for these trips was in July, August and September - the dry season. This was pretty much the rule for the eastern side of the mountains, although a little "iffy" to the west because of Pacific Ocean weather patterns, without the protective wall of the mountains to stop the moisture fall out. Snow depth at higher elevations in June was an obstacle at times.

The National Forest Service in the 1920's and earlier had constructed the main trail system that exists today, although some of the lesser trails they prepared have since been obliterated by logging roads or have been abandoned. The Forest Service was also responsible for the early shelters and enlisted the Civilian Conservation Corps (CCC) to provide trail building and maintenance, as well as additional shelter construction between 1933 and 1942.

The great bulk of this early construction, however, was achieved because of the efforts of early pioneer Chris Morgenroth. His Olympic experience began as a homesteader on the Bogachiel River in 1890, but in 1903 he was sworn in as a ranger in the Olympic Forest Reserve, later changed to the Olympic National Forest in 1905. He was directly responsible for the construction of all of the major river trails and shelters with connecting telephone lines prior to 1926, when he retired as Deputy Supervisor, Olympic National Forest. All of these trails and shelters were primarily to assist fire fighting crews, if needed, and secondarily for recreation. He was also responsible for much of the early coastal trail construction stretching from Forks to the Grays Harbor area, later to be upgraded and to become Highway 101.

In 1933 the Mt. Olympus National Monument was transferred from the National Forest Service to the National Park Service, and trail and shelter maintenance in the new Olympic National Monument had a new manager. Today the Park Service, probably because of budget restrictions, apparently no longer is maintaining the shelters and is in fact removing them. This probably makes sense to them as everyone today carries a mountain tent and stove, and the shelters have become obsolete. The traveling population was rather sparse in the early days and the shelters could accommodate everyone except for large parties such as boy scout troops or hiking clubs. Gatherings in the shelters would occasionally consist of several small parties of two or three members each, all sharing a common fire with room enough for everyone to have a dry bed. In dry weather each party usually preferred to make its own camp.

These shelters all seemed to fit a common design, although sometimes there were minor variations. They were, as I recall, about 14 feet by 16 feet with an eight or ten foot roof. One of the 16 foot sides was left open, and a fire pit was located on this, the front side. It had a shed roof, lower at the rear, and with a partial protective roof over the fire pit, leaving an opening at the peak to let smoke escape. Usually the three sides and roof were shingled with hand-hewn shakes.

Very few people carried tents in those days because of the extra weight. They stayed in the shelters instead if rain was expected. They did, however, usually carry a fairly large oilskin coat or similar garment to keep their pack dry while hiking, and to throw over part of their sleeping bag if caught in the rain.

Packs were usually of the homemade prospector or sourdough style. These were constructed of two wooden uprights held about 18 inches apart by cross members, and had a laced canvas cover to keep the framework from chafing the back of the bearer. Shoulder straps were secured to the top crossmember, then passed through a slit in the front of the canvas cover and over the shoulders. The ends of the straps terminated in adjustable buckles secured to the vertical side members. Screw hooks were fastened about six inches apart on each of the vertical members, thus allowing the bearer to lace a load on the pack with heavy cord. The load was prepared by placing a tarp, shelter half, blanket or other cover flat on the back of the empty pack, piling everything to be carried on the cover, folding the excess tops and sides of the cover over the board and then lacing the load securely to the board.

Some individuals preferred knapsacks to pack boards, but most people, I believe, considered them inadequate for large loads. They didn't carry enough, didn't balance properly, and sharp objects in the pack would always find their way into the middle of a person's back with aggravating results.

It was about this time that a new commercial pack board appeared on the market. It was the ***Trapper Nelson Board***, similar in design to the ***Sourdough Board,*** but much lighter, came in several sizes to fit the individual, and seemed to balance better. Another feature that was a major improvement was the use of a large sack secured to the board that eliminated all of the old fashioned lacings and allowed immediate access to the contents. The bag was removable and huge loads, if desired, could still be tied on.

Bedding in those days was usually one of three types. One of these was the typical commercial model sleeping bag. It consisted of an insulated blanket about 60 inches by 72 inches long, the insulation being either wool bat or kapok. One side of the blanket was covered with a waterproof duck material, and the whole blanket was folded in half, the duck cover on the outside, and the bottom and open side provided with a talon fastener for entrance, exit or ventilation. The duck cover was extended about 48 inches lengthwise on the underside of the bag at the opening end and provided a built-in tarp to cover the top of the bag in case of rain (or mosquitoes). Advertising illustrations depicted this added tarp as a little tent over the occupant's head, supported by small trimmed branches, to keep him dry. Unfortunately, it proved impossible to rig the tent and still get in or out of the bag. Assistance was required of a second party and, once inside, the occupant was afraid to move for fear of tearing down the tent. Under the circumstances, the call of nature would have to be deferred until morning.

A second type of bedding was the homemade sleeping bag, one which I used for about five years before I upgraded. This type consisted of a comforter similar to that in the commercial type, but with about a three-pound bat of wool covered with quilted flannel. After folding the material in half, the bottom and side were sewn together, except for about 18 inches at the top of the side which remained open for access. This was kept closed, if desired, with safety pins. A covering bag of unbleached muslin, with the added tarp was also added, if desired. The muslin cover was waterproofed as follows: about two pounds of paraffin was melted in a large pan on a stove, then removed to the outdoors and a gallon of gasoline mixed thoroughly with the melted paraffin. At this point the muslin cover was placed in the pan, thoroughly saturated with the paraffin and gasoline mixture, then hung up on a clothesline until all of the gasoline had evaporated and the paraffin solidified. A hot iron was then applied to the cover and the paraffin ironed into the cloth and seams. This was really waterproof, much better than the commercial bag. Thinking back, it still frightens me to think of the potential for a serious, even fatal fire.

The third type of bedding consisted of three World War I surplus army blankets, folded in thirds lengthwise and held in this configuration by horseblanket pins, heavy safety pins about four inches long. A person entered this by wriggling into the top, selecting the number of blanket layers he wanted on top or under him. This could be covered with a tarp, rain coat or whatever. Most of the individuals I knew who used blankets also made a waterproof cover similar to that described in the previous paragraph.

None of these types of bedding were very satisfactory in the rain. The first type usually leaked, as the duck waterproofing wasn't waterproof and the zipper always leaked. Of course, the little tent arrangement was also a disaster. The other two types proved better, and didn't leak for a year or two. Then the hard paraffin would crack, and the waterproofing had to be repeated. Of course, as it was really waterproof and vapor tight it held in body perspiration and ultimately made a damp bed if used too many nights without airing.

One of the principal problems of any of them was the inability to keep water from seeping underneath. This could be overcome if a thick bed of boughs was placed underneath. The sleeping bags in those days, if they had enough insulation to keep a person warm, were also quite heavy and bulky. The absence of a tent offset, to some extent, the weight of the sleeping bags, but required rainy nights to be spent in Forest Service shelters.

Some individuals were using World War I army surplus shelter halves (two of them, when buttoned together, made a two-man tent, but with no door or floor) and also served as covers for their sourdough packs. Thus, two people could have a tent. The problem was, most of the surplus shelter halves leaked badly.

Many of my friends and I, even in those days, managed to camp away from shelters and stay dry if we planned ahead sufficiently. We discovered that in heavy old growth timber where the trees were fairly close together there would actually be dry areas immediately next to some of those tree trunks. Cedar trees worked best, but spruce and fir were okay. We would occasionally get a drip, but nothing serious. At higher subalpine levels, it was amazing the number of dry places that could be found in spruce or fir thickets. Branches from larger trees, too, drooped down against the trunks and made excellent bivouacs between them.

Clothing was a serious subject to consider. Long sleeved shirts were common because of mosquitoes and flies, with a wool sweater for warmth. Long wool pants were preferred, although shorts were appearing in increasing numbers. A rainhat, raincoat and wind- breaker with hood filled out the wardrobe. Everyone wore two pairs of socks at a time - silk or rayon next to the foot and wool over. The theory was that all friction in the boot was between the two layers of socks and not your foot, thereby avoiding blisters. I guess it works.

Boots were usually heavy work boots with 8 inch tops. Two schools of thought prevailed regarding the soles. The climbers preferred thick leather soles that would hold climbing nails called *triconis*. A serious climber wouldn't be caught dead with anything else, as the edging nails enhanced photographs if shown on a boot hooked onto a small protuberance of a rock wall. They also weighed a lot. The other school, the hikers and fishermen, preferred rubber soles as they were lighter and usually gripped better on most surfaces. *Vibram* rubber soles had not yet been invented, although their use now is almost universal and a vast improvement.

The subject of food is always provocative, especially to those preparing menus for back packing trips. Our group preferred the following, more from a bulk and weight standpoint than taste, as they were all more or less palatable. There were no freeze-dried foods available, the cost of dehydrated foods was prohibitive, and so we bought off-the-shelf.

The following made up most of our meals:

Breakfast
rolled oats, dried prunes, sugar and
Eagle-brand canned milk
or
hot cakes with jam (not both)

Lunch
rye crisp or pilot bread and jam or cheese
candy bars

Dinner
Macaroni and cheese
or
Spaghetti with tomato sauce
or
Rice with dried prunes
and
Fish, if catchable, as a supplement to the above

Between meals
candy bars, cookies, etc.- the individual's choice

As can be seen, bulk was added from local water we mixed or cooked in, and was not packed from home. The danger of *Giardia* in the water was nonexistent, and the idea of carrying water bottles and sterilizing pills or pumps was inconceivable. All flowing water was "good" water.

Because we did not have small mountain stoves (they were available, we just couldn't afford them) we always carried a camp axe - one with at least a 24 inch handle. Hatchets just couldn't do the job. The axe was absolutely essential to get suitable fire wood. Another essential was a number of candle stubs, for use in fire building. Squaw brush, the small, dead branches near the ground on alpine spruce or fir trees would ignite and burn if enough heat could be generated, but matches just couldn't do it. If the wood was dry, matches would suffice, but it usually wasn't and fine shavings of inner dry wood in branches supplemented the squaw brush. The matches were kept in secure waterproof containers, and used sparingly.

Nearly everyone carried a sheathed, belt-mounted hunting knife. It was a sort of macho affectation, but when kept razor sharp was an essential supplement to the axe for fire building and other camp chores. A Swiss Army knife would have been more practical.

Virtually all of the equipment and camping practices described earlier are obsolete and nearly all of the shelters are gone. Today's modern equipment - ultra light mountain tents with equally light rain flies and mosquito-proof access, *Kelty*-type frame or internal frame packs, ultra light weight thermofill sleeping bags with thermopad insulating mats, mountain stoves, featherweight goretex rain gear, polypropylene underwear, light weight hiking boots - all of these things are a major improvement over the equipment listed earlier.

While there is a great deal of nostalgia attached to the "good old days," I am happy to say that I now own all of the above new state-of-the-art equipment. I use it every summer and am grateful that it lets me continue my rambles in the Olympics.

CHAPTER 3
EARLY SCOUTING

Boy Scouting has held a dominant role in hiking and camping in the Olympic Mountains since shortly after the turn of the century. It probably got its start through leadership by members of early mountaineering groups. Minutes of The Mountaineers indicate that in 1911 one of their outstanding members, Major Ingraham, organized the Boy Scouts of America in the Northwest and stated that scouting was "The greatest all-time feeder for true mountaineering."

Another outstanding example is that of Edmond S. Meany, a distinguished professor and administrator of the University of Washington, author and president of The Mountaineers. He was the leader of a Boy Scout troop that made the first ascent of Mt. Tom in 1914. Mt. Tom is the western end of the Mt. Olympus massif about two miles west of the West Peak.

The mountain was christened "Mt. Tom" by the scouts in the party for Harry "Tom" Martin, one of the scouts. Tom Martin was destined to have an extended scouting career, as he later became the second camp director at Camp Cleland (discussed later) and was a committee member of the BSA regional committee from 1958 to 1970. He also served a term as Washington State Treasurer.

While there were probably other hikes by individual troops similar to that led by Dr. Meany, more structured programs sponsored by the Boy Scout councils in the Puget Sound area were born. These councils provided organized summer camps, promoting outings in the Olympic mountains by experienced leaders, and served the scouts whose parent troops did not provide annual outings. It was also an additional prime experience for those scouts who were members of a troop that did have a summer hiking program. The history of these camps and sponsoring councils, together with some of their activities, are listed herewith.

EARLY HIKING IN THE OLYMPICS

CAMP PARSONS

The Seattle Area Council, BSA (now the Chief Seattle Council, BSA) serving the Greater Seattle area, Kitsap, Jefferson and Clallam counties, was the first to inaugurate a summer camp. Camp Parsons is located on Jackson's Cove on the west shore of Hood Canal, and opened for its first season in 1919, with transportation by boat to the site. An alternate method was a four mile hike north from the ferry terminal at Brinnon on Hood Canal along the west shore to Camp Parsons.

A two-week camp per period was provided, for $7.50 per week including waterfront activities, handicrafts and attainment of scouting ranks and badges. A four or five-day hike in the mountains, ranging from easy to difficult (summitting Mt. Olympus) was offered to every scout. This same basic program is offered today, with the more difficult hikes restricted to third and fourth year campers.

As early as the mid-1920's the Camp Parsons staff conducted an annual "Trans-Olympic" hike, starting at the camp and hiking all the way across the heart of the Olympic Mountains to the Pacific Ocean beaches. One of these was sponsored by the *Seattle Star*, a former major newspaper. In 1926 the *Seattle Star* carried day-to-day progress reports obtained by radio from the scouts on the trail. Camp Parsons is well and improving with age. Donations by former scouts and friends have made it possible to expand the size of the camp and make necessary improvements. Camp directors for those early years were:

H.B. "Harry" Cunningham	Stuart P. Walsh
H. Glover Clark	L.S."Loody" Cristofero
W.D. "Ronsy" Rounsavell	Robert S. Lamm

May Camp Parsons continue to grow and improve, under leadership as perceptive and innovative as the above directors and all who followed have been.

CAMP CLELAND

The Tumwater Area Council, BSA, was founded in 1925, and was the governing body for scout troops from Mason, Lewis and

Thurston Counties. It has since been merged with Tacoma and Twin Harbors and is now known as Pacific Harbors Council, BSA. Max G. Stroup was the first scout executive. The initial council camping committee members were J.W. Davis, I. Ned Wood, Henry Brewer and Hans Cleland, who was also the first council president. These were the people who envisioned a summer camp for summer scouting activities and were responsible for the existence of Camp Cleland. Camp Cleland, named after Hans Cleland, an Olympia attorney, operated from the 1920's to the early 1940's when World War II gas rationing and other shortages forced its closure despite its 99-year Forest Service lease.

The site for the camp, at Lower Lake Lena in the Hamma Hamma river watershed, was obtained through the efforts of Wayne Sanders, a 16-year-old Eagle Scout from Tumwater who was working summers for the Hamma Hamma Logging Company in the Hamma Hamma valley. He was aware that the Tumwater Council was looking for a Tumwater Area Council permanent summer camp site and mentioned this to his supervisor. This ultimately led to an offer by the Hamma Hamma Logging Company to the Council of Lower Lake Lena for the camp site. The council accepted the offer and opened its first camp in 1927 - five 12-day periods per summer at $8.50 per period.

Travel to camp for the participating scouts was varied, exciting and a bit of an effort. It consisted of automobile transportation to Eldon, a small community on the west side of Hood Canal. Here they transferred to a Hamma Hamma Logging Company railroad scooter that carried them up the Hamma Hamma river to the trailhead of the route to the camp on Lower Lake Lena. A four and a half mile hike began with a steep grade and ended at Camp Cleland on the west bank of the lake, a gain of 700 feet in altitude. The boys carried all their personal items in backpacks, and food, equipment and similar items were transported by pack mules from the trailhead to the camp.

The first camp director was the council scout executive, Max Stroup, and his camp counselors were Norman Bright, Earl Hardy, Flash Partlow and Phil Bailey. The second camp director was Harry "Tom" Martin (of Mt.Tom fame). Another counselor in the early thirties was Chet Ullin, a college football player and mountain climber. Chet did a lot of pioneering hikes in the Hamma Hamma valley, and I can remember one incident that shows the extent of his enthusiasm.

I think it was in 1934 that I made a weekend hike in to visit Chet. When I arrived I was informed that Chet was on a five-day hike, but was expected back with a dozen or so scouts later in the day. Sure enough, here they came. They were singing one of the camp songs and it was obvious they were proud of the hike just ending. I can remember one of the smaller scouts commenting "Boy, did we charge through a lot of devils club." They had completely circled the upper Hamma Hamma valley, passing upper Lake Lena, Deerheart Lake, two small lakes on a Boulder Creek tributary (now called Stone Ponds), over St. Peter's Gate east of Mt. Stone, then Lake of the Angels, the east slopes of Mts. Skokomish and Henderson, then to Mildred Lakes, Jefferson Lake, and back to Camp Cleland - a fantastic feat for a truly pioneering effort! It had never been done before.

I read a short article by Ira Spring in *"Island of Rivers,"* an anthology celebrating 50 years of Olympic National Park. In reading Ira's article *Mountains, Cameras and Scouting,* I was surprised to find that he was one of the scouts on this trip.

The ultimate hike of every camp year was the "Titus Expedition," a hike so named in honor of Leon Titus, a member of the Tumwater Council Executive Board. This hike required that all participants be at least 14 years of age and have attended at least one previous season at camp. It was a two-week expedition and made great pioneering trips throughout the Olympics, encompassing such feats as a Mt. Olympus traverse, off-trail exploring from the Elwha to the Enchanted Valley and others.

But, to return to Camp Cleland on Lower Lena Lake. As the years passed Camp Cleland increased in popularity, but so did the interest in logging the Lake Lena area. The Forest Service had plans for this project when Norman Bright became aware of it. Through his efforts the Forest Service desisted, saving the camp. World War II presented extremely difficult management problems, and the camp closed in 1941. The camp, however, is not forgotten. Mounted on an outcropping rock near the former camp site is a plaque with the following words:

EARLY SCOUTING

"In memory of the scouts and leaders of Lena Lake's
Camp Cleland 1927 to 1941
Tumwater Council BSA
'Where our youth learned to appreciate our
outdoor heritage'"

CAMP BALDY

Scouting in the Twin Harbor area had its beginning in 1925 under the guidance of Elvis Eaton, the first scout executive of a brand new BSA Council, the Twin Harbors Council, BSA, covering all scouting activities in the Grays Harbor and Pacific counties. It has since been integrated with and is a part of the Pacific Harbors Council, BSA.

One of the major activities of scouting, particularly in the summer, is outdoor camping and hiking, and this area provided great opportunities for these pursuits. Nearly all BSA councils establish summer camps to accomplish these objectives, and what better place could be found than on the forested shores of Lake Quinault, a scant 20 miles by road from Hoquiam and Aberdeen? Elvis Eaton was able to secure a site for this future camp on the north shore of the lake. Because it was within a day's hike of Mt. Baldy, a popular local peak, the camp was given the name "Camp Baldy."

The initial group of scouts to attend the camp, under the supervision of Elvis Eaton, did a large part of the work in developing the camp. Trees and brush were cleared to make room for sleeping tents, a cooking shelter was erected and a swimming and boating waterfront was developed. After toilet pits were excavated and clean water facilities achieved the camp was in business, and all through the efforts of the participating scouts! Once the camp was established, Elvis Eaton, doing double duty as Camp Director and Scout Executive, trained assistants and camp counselors. For the first year or two activities consisted of camping and woodcraft skills, pursuing merit badge and rank achievements and improving swimming and boating skills. In addition, day hikes were scheduled to climb Mt. Baldy and nearby Mt. Colonel Bob. Overnight hikes were also made by the older scouts to Elk Lake and up both branches of the Quinault River. Later, more ambitious activities were planned and executed. Extended hiking and climbing expeditions, some of them of a week's duration, were carried out. Jim Stewart, one of the early Camp Baldy scout residents (now a practicing attorney in Montesano) and Ed Maxie (now a retired banker in Aberdeen) were members of an ambitious trek in the early thirties - to climb Mt. Olympus. About 10 or 15 older scouts, led by a Mr. Hamilton, traveled north on the Skyline trail (a route along the crest of the ridge between the Queets and Quinault watersheds). When they reached Lake Beauty they left the established trail and continued along the ridge, consecutively climbing Mt. Noyes, Mt. Meany and Mt. Queets, then dropping down into the Queets Basin. All of this with heavy backpacks! They established a base camp there under a protective overhang of rock, calling it the Boy Scouts' Shelter Rock. The next day, with lightened packs, they climbed out of the Basin to Humes Glacier, bivouacking for the night on Blizzard Pass, the divide between the Humes and Hoh Glaciers. As Ed Maxey said, *"There wasn't much room on the ridge and it was pretty steep down both sides. We didn't roll around much that night."* In the morning, the scouts climbed down 700 feet to the Hoh Glacier, crossed it to Glacier Pass, then down Blue Glacier to the Snow Dome. Their route then led up the Snow Dome and ultimately to the summit of Mt. Olympus' West Peak.

Return was made the same day, following the same route, all the way to Shelter Rock Camp. Two more days on the trail and they reached Camp Baldy, having crossed Dodwell-Rixon Pass, the Low Divide, and 16 more miles of trail. Apparently the scouting activities later took a new trend, and ultimately hiking in the Olympics was dropped. A new camp site was selected, and Camp Delezenne, located near Elma, took its place about 1950. The backpacking treks into the Olympic Mountains ceased.

Although the Twin Harbors district camp activities have drifted away from Olympic Mountains exploration, individual troops still are pursuing these activities, notably by Montesano Troop No. 16 and its leader Jack Boyer. Hopefully, the mystical call of the Olympics will be passed on to future scouts with programs similar to those that were provided by Camp Baldy.

SECTION I

Major River Trails - Elwha, Dosewallips, Duckabush and Quinault

CHAPTER 4
A WEEK TO REMEMBER

A scout's first organized, extended backpacking trek presents a lot of new experiences, all of them exciting, some of them awesome. One of the major lessons is the art of hiking with a heavy pack (a tedious chore) while at the same time having pleasant thoughts about the unusual scenic views, the expectant dinner in camp, a story to tell a friend - anything to divert thoughts from a tired back. The ambition to reach a certain trail destination also makes the physical effort worth while. Once a person learns to enjoy the mountain experience, the back packing no longer is drudgery, but part of the whole experience. (This same mental acceptance of a heavy pack is, of course, applicable to all who enjoy the mountains).

A description of typical day-to-day events and activities that occur on an extended Olympics scout hike are related here that I as a tenderfoot experienced on my first annual Troop 503 hike. This was in July, 1931 and actually started in the basement of the Methodist Church in Bremerton the evening before our departure for the mountains.

Our scoutmaster was "Heinie" Strehlau, who was able to make our activities, at home and on the trail both fun and a learning process at the same time. His assistant was Gordie Hudson, another great guy who really went out of his way to explain things to the younger scouts so that they understood them and the reason for them. He had also come up through the ranks and appreciated a lot of the crazy things we did.

A list of required items to be carried by each scout had been handed out at a previous meeting and tonight, the night before departure, an inspection was held to be sure all scouts were properly equipped. In addition to clothing there were included packboards, sleeping bags or blankets and shelter halves (a half of a pup tent). An inspection of every item of clothing and equipment for each boy was made to make sure essentials were there and excess items deleted to save weight. When all of this had been accomplished the food, cooking utensils and common camp items such as an axe, first aid equipment and cook pots were distributed among scouts unequally to insure that the smallest boys did not get a large addition. The leaders and older boys carried the major load.

With a final warning that the expedition would leave the front of the church at 8:00 a.m. sharp - so everybody would be there no later than 7:00 a.m. after a good breakfast and with a brown bag lunch - we said goodnight and went home to spend a restless night thinking about the next day.

There were about 20 of us making the hike, and we were all there on time. It was drizzling slightly as we climbed aboard the tarp-covered flatbed stake truck, sat down with our packs on the hay-covered bottom, and spent the next three or four hours in noisy talking and singing. We were really ready for the trek. We rounded Hood Canal, passed Quilcene, Sequim, Port Angeles and finally turned up the Elwha River to the trailhead at Whiskey Bend. The precipitation had ended, and we all got out of the truck and headed for the woods to make ourselves more comfortable, and then had our lunch of sandwiches we had brought from home. As some had already been into their lunches while in the truck and were still hungry, we who hadn't eaten yet had to guard our's while we ate them.

After lunch we were ready, and lining up we hoisted packs and started out after Gordie, with Heinie bringing up the rear. We were still hyped up from our truck ride and continued singing songs for about a mile when the noise and laughter slowly decreased in volume. After a period of silence a plaintive voice was heard to ask "how much farther to camp?" A rest was called, and after a reasonable time Gordie explained customs of the trail: no one complained unless there was a legitimate reason, such as the suspected formation of a blister or the need to repack a disintegrating packboard. From then on things went reasonably well with frequent rest stops and only a couple of suspected blister problems. The tenderfeet (including me), a minority, were the ones who had to learn the rules of the road.

Our trail had passed through open meadows near the river with lots of big timber farther away. It had been an up and down situation with some hills up over obstructions and then down to the flats along the river again. We passed several rough cabins which appeared to be vacant and finally arrived at our destination for that day, Camp Lillian at the junction of Lillian River with the Elwha River. We had traveled four miles. There were high banks alongside the Lillian River, heavily timbered and there was quite a drop down to the river. Very little sunshine got down to our campsite through the large trees, leaving a rather melancholy atmosphere.

After a short relaxing period to unwind, Heinie suggested that we prepare camp for the night, so flat places on the forest floor suitable for pitching the pup tents were searched out and utilized. It immediately appeared that there was a shortage of such places until Gordie took the homeless under his wing and found them satisfactory spots to bed down. The next order was to gather firewood, and everyone scattered through the adjacent forest to collect the driest they could find. As this was a popular camp site we had to move away from camp, but it was plentiful at a distance. For the first night, Heinie and Gordy made the cooking fire and prepared the first meal of the trip.

While this was taking place everyone else had a free period, and with admonitions to stay with his buddy everyone was on his own. This was a great opportunity to go fishing, and my friend Bob "Pete" Pedersen and I went down to the mouth of the Lillian River and found that small cutthroat liked salmon eggs, so we proceeded to catch at least half a dozen. Some of the others were also fishing, and between us we must have had a couple of dozen trout. When Gordie learned of this he immediately decided they were just what the rice he was cooking needed to add flavor, so in the pot went the trout.

Dinner was served by Gordie, spooned out of a huge cookpot. The rice was supplemented by bread and butter and cocoa, and the milk for the cocoa was diluted *Eagle Brand* canned milk. After dinner one of the three patrols in the troop was designated by Heinie to wash the community pots and pans and to be responsible for the next day's fire and breakfast. Dishwashing consisted of taking the pots and pans to the river and scouring them with beach sand, rinsing them and letting them air dry until breakfast. Everyone was responsible for his own utensils.

The campfire that night was a much anticipated event, as Gordy was a marvelous story teller, and we looked forward to them. In addition to stories were songs, some old and some new that Gordie had picked up just for this trip. There were many questions regarding the day's hike and camp preparation, and then Heinie outlined the next day's trek and what to expect, as well as further suggestions to make things more fun for everyone. Gordy led us in the closing song we sang at every gathering. It is a wonderful thing, and even without the music here it is:

Softly dims the light of day
as our campfire fades away;
Silently each scout should ask
"Have I done my daily task?
Have I kept my honor bright?
Can I guiltless face the night?
Have I done and have I dared
everything to be prepared?"

Thus, a reminder of the scouting ethic ended our first day on the trail. Gordy woke us up early the next day, sounding the call by beating on a cook pot with a stick. The patrol having the duty was busy getting the cooking fire going when Gordie pulled from his pack a couple of dozen eggs he had carefully packed in. He also had bacon, as well as bread and butter, so we really had a fine breakfast. Gordie warned us, however, that there were no more goodies in his pack and that from here on we would have the same breakfast every morning - cooked oatmeal and dried prunes with sugar and Eagle Brand milk. There were no complaints then because we were still enjoying today. It would be a different story on the morrow, however.

After breakfast we cleaned up the camp to leave no debris or garbage for the next camper, and after packing everything started up the trail, the next stop to be Elkhorn Camp. It was really a tough climb up out of the Lillian River, but once we were up it was a pretty good trail, still in big timber, but with only minor ups and downs. At lunchtime we sat on the bank of the Elwha and had lunch - little packs of rye-crisp with jam, the same lunch we would have for the next week. There was some muttering among the tenderfeet, but none from the older boys who already knew what it would be. Some of them, however, had bootlegged candy bars to supplement their lunch, and very jealously ate them in private.

We arrived at Elkhorn in the middle of the afternoon after having traveled about seven miles and camp was made in the same manner as the previous night. The campsite here was much different than the one at Lillian River, as there was a large cleared meadow next to the river and the whole area was open. Wood for fire was secured and another patrol was assigned to fire and cooking duty for tonight and tomorrow morning. The menu for dinner was spaghetti and canned spaghetti sauce, and while it was being prepared (supervised by Gordy) the rest of us went fishing again with about the same luck. The fish were small, but plentiful, and they were added to the spaghetti and helped to appease our appetites. An appetite is definitely stimulated after hiking seven miles with a pack!

Early in the evening the sky became overcast, and Gordie declared that we should put all of the wood we had gathered inside the three-sided Forest Service shelter and to be sure that everything was inside our tents. We were also cautioned to be sure our tents weren't located in hollows that would gather water and run under our sleeping bags. This caused a search for more adequate ground in some cases, but everyone was ready for rain by campfire time.

When we went to bed it had started to sprinkle and the sound of rain falling in the forest added to the roar of the river, and we congratulated ourselves upon having made such a dry camp. It wasn't long though before the sound of the rain drowned out that of the river, and we experienced a regular cloudburst. By morning there were a number of wet scouts, rated from minor damp to heavy saturation. The experienced Gordie had foreseen some of this and, thus, our fairly dry supply of firewood inside the shelter. All those who were wet brought their sleeping bags into the shelter and then began an all-day drying operation by the fire. Those who were more fortunate helped to relocate wet tents, and members of the duty patrol who were not drying their belongings got breakfast. It soon stopped raining and a short while later the sun came out, supplementing the drying operation and clearing out the extremely crowded conditions inside the shelter. Two adjacent fire pits were used as additional drying sites. As Heinie had decided we would not move camp that day, those not on the drying detail could do other things. Pete and I went fishing again with the same results. I decided to change off from the salmon egg bait I had been using and switched to various types of bugs I could find. They all worked to some extent, but the black beetles the ranger on the Dosewallips had shown me many years ago still worked best. Our catch was added to the dinner the next patrol was preparing. The menu was macaroni and cheese, and Gordie wasn't sure that it would add to the flavor, but we reminded him that it made up in volume what it lacked in flavor, and he capitulated.

By this time most of the sleeping bags had dried out sufficiently to be usable and we proceeded to have a campfire. Afterward those with leaky shelter halves slept in the shelter with Heinie and Gordie and those with watertight halves who had lost their "leaky" buddies teamed up with those with dry halves. As we climbed into bed the stars were out in great numbers, and we looked forward to a good day on the morrow.

At the campfire Heinie had said we only had about six miles to go to our next campsite at Hayes River, and that it should be a fairly easy trail, so when we got up in the morning to sunshine everyone was eager to be on the move. Complaints about the oatmeal were nonexistent and after the camp site cleanup and packing we were off to singing, whistling and lots of laughter.

We arrived at Hayes River camp after an uneventful, cheerful hike through more large timbered areas, and went about normal preparations for camp. The first patrol to draw duty was back on (my turn again) and the menu was rice and fishheads again, as the fishermen again did their thing. Those with still damp bags meanwhile finished the drying process. Particular pains were taken this time to locate the best possible tent sites, and those with leaky tents continued to sleep in the shelter. Heinie's description for our next day's hike was long and uphill, a distance of about 10 miles. It would be the hardest day of the whole trip, so in the morning we would recheck everyone's pack and redistribute loads so that the weight was equally distributed among the scouts.

The next day was warm and sunny and everyone was in good spirits. The backpacking of our previous days had toughened us up so that we had no malingerers and after readjusting pack weights we started up the trail. It began with a couple of switchbacks, then took off in a steady sidehill climb through timber on the north side of the Hayes River. Gordie was in the lead and held us down to a very slow, but steady pace that fit our physical abilities, making rest stops about every 30 minutes with not a complaint. Our only problem was the shortage of drinking water, and this was solved about four or five miles up the trail when we crossed a small stream and decided to have lunch.

There were no audible comments about our "rye-crisp jam cake," and we started again up the trail. It was about here that we broke out of the dense trees and into subalpine meadows and groups of white fir. The wildflowers were out in abundance, and I recalled another display when as a small child I traveled through similar meadows on Mt. Ellinor. I was once again fascinated by their beauty and fairylike atmosphere and my hiking aches had somehow disappeared. The sun was shining, we were above timberline, and I was in Heaven.

Our wonderland trail continued to climb through these meadows and topped out at Hayden Pass, the low spot in the ridge between the Dosewallips and Elwha Rivers. On this ridge to the north of Hayden Pass was Mt. Claywood and to the south was Sentinal Peak. This was a logical time to stop and enjoy the wonderful scenery displayed all around us. Gordie suggested that we climb Sentinal Peak, which was close at hand and an easy scramble. The climb was as easy as he said it would be, and the view from the summit was outstanding.

We were all familiar with the skyline of the Olympic Mountains from the East - the spectacular view of Mt. Ellinor, Mt. Washington, The Brothers and Mt. Constance. Now we were seeing these same peaks from the West, plus all of the intervening peaks as well as the entire Dosewallips valley and Silt Creek. To the south, Mt. Anderson and its partner West Anderson were separated by Eel Glacier, the source of Silt Creek's water. Flypaper pass, the lowest notch in the ridge between Mt. Anderson and West Anderson, lay at the very top of Eel Glacier. This area completely fascinated me, and I vowed someday to come back and explore all this country between Hayden Pass and Eel Glacier.

As it was growing late in the day we once again put on our packs and started down the Dosewallips trail to the Thousand Acre Meadow and Dose Meadows. The Thousand Acre Meadow was a huge, relatively flat alpine meadow just a few hundred feet down the trail from Hayden Pass, and we found an excellent camp ground in the meadow a few feet from the Dosewallips River. Actually, a person could jump across it at this point as it flowed from a snowbank. This was the first snow we had been able to approach, although a number of snowdrifts had been visible from our great view at the pass.

Signpost at Hayden Pass.

Camp was set up, and a supply of wood for the fire was gathered by everyone, although this was a little difficult as we had to travel quite a distance to reach downed trees and branches that were suitable. We were almost above timberline and only a few groups of alpine firs or spruce were within reach. We were suddenly surprised by the shrill whistle of a marmot. A lot of younger scouts had never heard the distinctive whistle before and eagerly looked at the source, pointed out by Gordie.

The sun set early as Mt. Claywood to the west blocked out the late afternoon sun, and it immediately began to get cold. We had a campfire, but everyone was tired, it was cold, and bed seemed like a good idea. So ended our fifth day of the hike.

The temperature dropped dramatically that night, and there were very few of us who didn't suffer. The next morning, fortunately, the sun was up quite early, there being no mountains to shield it, and things warmed up right away. After breakfast a snowball fight erupted between patrols, but didn't last very long as Gordie organized things to do.

We hiked back up to Hayden pass (without packs) and climbed Mt. Claywood, another easy peak that gave us a different perspective as we could look north toward the Straights of Juan De Fuca and see an entirely different group of mountains. While still at Hayden Pass we observed three deer grazing in the meadows below, and as we descended they watched us, but didn't run away, finally moving off further down the meadow. After the return to camp from this climb we had lunch, explored the Thousand Acre Meadow some more, and Heinie suggested that we hike on down the trail to a lower elevation where it would be warmer at night. This was a great idea, so down the trail we went.

The descent didn't take us very long as it was only about two miles, but we had dropped in elevation from about 5,300 feet to about 4,500 feet and the trail had changed.

We still had meadows, but they were interspersed with groups of alpine trees, and among them we found

Hayden Pass looking east.

a campsite that was ideal for our use and we proceeded to occupy it. Activities in this camp consisted mainly of exploration, and Pete and I and some of the others climbed the ridge to the north through meadows, and dropping down the other side came across a small lake with a snowbank on one side. It looked like a pretty good place to go swimming so we jumped out of our clothes and into the lake. Needless to say, once was enough, and one of the others told me I was out of the lake so fast that the bottoms of my feet didn't even get wet!

After exploring around a bit more we discovered that a black bear about a hundred yards away was standing still and staring at us. This made us decide immediately that it was about time to return to camp and go fishing. This turned out a loser, as no one had a single strike and we didn't stay with it very long.

Sleeping conditions that night were a great improvement over the night before although some of us were still cold. Morning was again warm and sunny, and we were virtually overflowing with energy as we left Dose Meadows and hiked down the trail to our next destination, the junction of the Dosewallips River and the West Fork of the Dosewallips at a campground named the Forks Camp. Camp was set up and Heinie made a speech. He mentioned (as we all knew) that the next day would be the end of the trip, and we would meet our parents at the Elkhorn Campground for a big "welcome back picnic."

That last night's campfire was wonderful. We sang the usual songs and heard stories, but in addition each patrol had to put on a skit highlighting some event that had taken place on the hike, but preferably amusing. Heinie made another little speech stating that this had been the best outing the troop had ever made (despite the rainy night) and that he was proud of us.

The hike to Elkhorn Campground was uneventful, although there was lots of talk about what a great picnic we would have, with all of that wonderful food that only Mom knew how to do. The picnic was everything we anticipated.

As we drove back to Bremerton in my folks' brand new Model-A Ford, I thought back over the 1931 troop 503 annual Olympics hike and hoped that there would be more, even better ones.

CHAPTER 5
VALLEY OF 1000 WATERFALLS

In June, 1935, our class graduated from Bremerton High School and we, the graduates, all seemed to immediately take divergent paths; some on vacation, some to jobs, and some to just disappear, out of contact. I, too, had a job beginning in July, but I certainly didn't want to hang around town until then with nothing to do. It was a beautiful June, the sun was causing the snow capped Olympics to outdo themselves in trying to lure me with all their charms, and I became their willing victim.

It was rather frustrating to search for others at this point in their careers who could drop everything for a trip to the hills, at least in early June, but I was finally successful. Most of those I contacted were obligated until later in the summer, but there were two with desires similar to mine and who shared my thoughts. These were Bill Eldridge and Ray Layton. They were enthusiastic over the idea of an early season hike in the Olympics.

We met one evening at my house and made all our plans, including our itinerary. I also got my father's promise to drive us to the trailhead on the Duckabush River two days later, after his shift in the Puget Sound Navy Yard ended. According to schedule, we were all waiting, with our packs. Right after work, dad picked us up and we were off. The trip was uneventful and we ultimately found ourselves at the end of the road, alone, in a Forest Service shelter full of rats. This was our first night away.

We hadn't anticipated the rats, but having read about their behavior we put all of our food in one of the packs, suspended it with wire someone had left, probably after using it as we were doing. We then went many feet away from the shelter to sleep, free of the rascals. The next morning there were lots of rat signs, but all of our food was still secure, and we proceeded with our oatmeal breakfast.

We were off to a fairly early start as we figured we had about eight miles to travel that day. Our route took us over Little Hump, and the trail didn't fool around, climbing steeply for about half a mile, then abruptly dropping again back to the river. Another fairly flat hike following the river led us to the next nuisance, the Big Hump. The trail abruptly started up a series of switchbacks, quite a few more than we had experienced on Little Hump. We finally topped out and immediately started down on the other side with more switchbacks. It appeared to us a very discouraging way for the Olympics to greet us after all their wiles to get us there.

Once the two humps were behind us, however, things improved remarkably and the trail followed the river through a forest of huge old growth timber in a gradual ascent. We soon came to Five Mile camp with its typical Forest Service shelter and stopped long enough to have a couple of candy bars apiece, our lunch.

The night stop was to be Ten Mile camp so we knew we had another five miles more. Bill was eager to get there and enjoy some of the good fishing he had heard about on the Duckabush so set a pace that got us there a couple of hours later. Fishing wasn't too good and we caught only one trout between us. The river was too high due to early season snow melting.

Ten Mile camp also had a Forest Service shelter, and although we saw no signs of either rats or mice we suspended our food as we had the night before. In the morning there was our usual hot oatmeal, but we spiked it with the one fish from yesterday's catch. It made a strange combination, but really wasn't too bad.

Our next stop was scheduled to be Camp Duckabush where the trail to First Divide branched off to the south and our trail continued on up the Duckabush River. It was about an eight mile hike, not too strenuous, and we were there shortly after noon. It was necessary to cross the river to get to the Camp Duckabush shelter and there was no bridge. After searching futilely for a handy log crossing we resigned ourselves to wading. Taking off our socks, we climbed back into our shoes and through knee deep water that tried desperately to carry us down stream we successfully made the passage.

VALLEY OF 1000 WATERFALLS

Fishing had been on the agenda for the afternoon, but high water changed that. Ray had planned to hike on up to the First Divide on an exploring expedition while Bill and I fished, so we decided to join Ray. It was about three miles to the divide and, after suspending our food in the shelter, we left for the divide with dry socks and wet boots.

It was uphill all the way, and we hadn't climbed very far when snow drifts appeared, eventually making 100 percent ground cover. In areas where the sun reached it, the going was quite difficult because of soft snow, and we were happy to finally gain the summit. There was snow all around us and we knew we were there too early in the year. The lovely meadows covered with wild flowers would not appear until much later.

It was still winter at this elevation and looking to the west we saw where an avalanche had made its way down the east side of Mt. Steel. Mt. Hopper was dominant to the east, and to the south we could see the North Fork Skokomish Valley, with Mt.Skokomish in the near foreground. As we started on our way back over the snow fields we could see Mt. LaCrosse and Mt.White directly ahead of us.

It had been a long, tiring day and because of the side trip in the snow we had very wet boots, socks and pant legs. Drying these, then, consumed the rest of the day and evening. Dinner turned out to be our favorite dish - macaroni and cheese - and with the sun long since out of sight over the LaCrosse Basin to the west we went to bed.

The following day we continued on up the Duckabush River, always climbing, high on the south side. A mile or two of this, and we dropped down to cross the river. Here again we had to wade, up to our knees again, in a very swift current. It was not easy, as a slip would mean a rather hazardous exercise in self-rescue and a thorough soaking. Fortunately we all made it, and after putting our socks on again continued up the trail. Actually, there was no trail - just snow drifts. This was just like yesterday's climb, except that we had our heavy packs with us to compound the problem. We were sinking very deeply into the snow now and it was well after lunchtime when we stumbled across a snow field to Marmot Lake and dropped our packs at the Forest Service shelter there.

Although we had travelled less than four miles, we knew that we wouldn't get much farther that day. It was obvious that if we were to continue through O'Neil Pass and drop down to the East Fork Quinault River the next day we would have to be fresh and well rested. Sitting around the shelter after about an hour became quite boring, though, as the weather was beautiful and Heart and LaCrosse Lakes were calling us. After experimenting with local snow travel we found that on the level, with one person breaking trail and the others using his footprints it wasn't too bad as long as we switched off in breaking trail. We didn't generate any speed, but we did manage to explore the La Crosse Basin.

The trails were all covered by snow, of course, so we could decide our own route. This was basically a straight line up a steep slope to the north where we reached Heart Lake after about half a mile of slow going. The lake was completely frozen over, and the difficulty of travel precluded any exploration, so we moved on northerly in fairly level terrain up the valley a mile or so to Lake LaCrosse at the head of the cirque. This lake was originally named by Lt. O'Neil's party "The Lake of the Holy Cross" and was so named because of the apparent configuration of a snag on the shore in the shape of a cross. Snow again was our enemy and, upon reaching this lake, we stopped briefly and then followed our footsteps back to the shelter at Marmot Lake.

We could all visualize what LaCrosse Basin could be like later

Marmot Lakes.

in the summer, with the snow gone and all of the many meadows luxuriously showing off the scores of different species of wild flowers. We realized that our early summer trip had been ill-timed, and we had missed the great flower show. Regrettably, as far as I was concerned, the marvelous meadows I had fallen in love with as a small child on Mt. Ellinor were one of the major attractions of the Olympics. However, we were there in June and must make the most of it.

Mt. Steel to the south rose impressively and southwest through O'Neil Pass we could see the East Fork Quinault River Valley leading in a southerly direction to Lake Quinault and the Pacific Ocean. To the east was the Duckabush River Valley we had just ascended to its headwaters here in the LaCrosse Basin. This made it all worth while, and we didn't regret our decision to come.

The outlet to Marmot Lake was open, and we had no difficulty in obtaining water. Wood, though, was a different story. We all spread out and traveled quite a distance in order to find enough squaw brush for our evening and breakfast cooking fires. After all this was accomplished, we proceeded to get dinner, but didn't have enough firewood to dry clothes or shoes.

The Enchanted Valley in the East Fork Quinault River was to be our camp the next day, so we were up very early and ready to be on our way while the snow surface was still firm from the cold night we had just experienced. There were a couple of miles to O'Neil Pass, and the overnight hardening of the snow hadn't helped much. It's advantage was gone shortly after we left the shelter. There was nothing for it but to post-hole our way up the fairly mild grade to the pass, the notch in the ridge to the west. With packs we were sinking in from six to eight inches every step and, of necessity, were pulling our feet out vertically this same amount every step. Travel was extremely slow, even with alternating leaders, and it was the middle of the day when we reached the pass.

A major rest stop was called at the pass, and after a couple of candy bars to keep us going we discussed our route from this point. We had hoped to follow remnants of the O'Neil party's trail in 1890, but the snow had obliterated all traces and we could find no blazes on the few trees there were. We finally decided we should just go more or less straight down the valley wall to the Quinault River we could barely hear far below us.

This plan was no sooner made than executed. We still had deep snow, but we were on a steep grade and the going was easier. Soon we came across bare patches and, after dropping down about a 1,000 feet or so, were back in dense timber and no snow. Our traveling problems were changing, but were not much better. We now faced a very steep grade requiring local underbrush to offer handholds so we could control our rate of descent. Further, there was an abundance of fallen trees that we must crawl under or over, and travel was slow.

Although we had anticipated game trails, these didn't materialize. Late in the afternoon we gave up the battle. We were completely exhausted, hungry and above all thirsty. The sound of the Quinault River below us had appreciably increased in volume, however, and the Enchanted Valley cliffs across the river certainly appeared closer. We split up our party, with Ray staying with the packs while Bill traveled south in search of a stream, or water of any sort. I traveled north on a similar mission, but neither of us had any luck. We kept shouting to keep in touch with Ray, and when we got to the extreme edge of sound communication went a few yards beyond, then turned back until we once again heard Ray's voice.

When we were all together again we decided to continue our drop to the river. This was an abortive attempt, however, as in our exhausted condition the going became dangerous. We ultimately gave up, each of us found a relatively flat nest on the uphill side of our own private tree and went to bed in a dry camp, candy bars our only food.

The next morning at dawn found us on our way again, much stronger, but very thirsty. It took us another two hours to reach the Quinault River, and the first thing we did was make a valiant attempt to drink the river dry. Our dehydration was great, and it took quite awhile for us to make the effort to cross the river to its west side where the river trail was in plain sight. We split up again, and about 500 yards north I found a sizeable log that gave access to the Quinalt Trail.

Immediately adjacent to the trail was a gravel bar, and our next chore was a fire and a huge pot of hot rolled oats. As much as I disliked the monotonous breakfast we had every day, it tasted great on this occasion. When breakfast was behind us we were off again up the trail.

Three miles later the Enchanted Valley Chalet came into view in a large river bottom meadow, and we stopped to explore. We were in what has been called "The Valley of 1000 Waterfalls" and the name was certainly appropriate. Water was cascading off the canyon walls, particularly the west side, in many cascades, and the indescribable site was at its peak because of the heavy June snow melt. It must have been well before the tourist season as it was unoccupied and boarded up.

After yesterday's and this morning's exertion we were none of us in the mood to travel farther that day, so left our packs at the chalet and just enjoyed a leisurely rest. The sun finally looked over the east valley rim and its wonderful rays did much to reenergized us.

Valley of 1000 Waterfalls (Enchanted Valley).

Ray went for a hike up the valley, and Bill and I went fishing. I couldn't find any of my little black beetles, but we did all right anyway with salmon eggs and by dinnertime had enough fish for a complete meal. This was quite puzzling, as the Quinalt River was as high as the Duckabush, but the fish were biting.

We cleaned them, then skewered them on willow sticks and roasted them like hot dogs. You had to be quick to pull them away from the fire, though, as they tended to get soft when done and to fall off the stick. This happened to a couple of them but we managed to rescue and eat them, charcoal and all. That night we slept in a woodshed located adjacent to the chalet (there was no Forest Service lean-to). The next day, still with cloudless skies, we started up the trail for Anderson Pass, a distance of about four miles. We anticipated more snow at the pass, and it was there. It first appeared about two miles up the trail, just as Ray had reported. Because of the heavy tree cover and natural shade for this portion of the trail it was quite firm until we broke out of the timber and even then was not nearly as difficult as we had expected.

Until we lost a day's travel time getting to the Enchanted Valley Chalet, we had planned to take a day to climb Mt. Anderson. This was now out of the question. Besides, snow conditions in Flypaper Pass would probably be impossible because of avalanche hazards anyway. The rest of the day was spent in a leisurely walk down the West Fork Dosewallips River. We ran out of snow at Honeymoon Meadows, and the now clear trail made things easier.

We camped that night in the Forest Service shelter at Diamond Meadows. The night brought the end of our clear, sunshiny weather. We awoke to a high overcast and decided we had better head for home before the weather broke. We started down the trail with our goal the Elkhorn Ranger Station that evening. This meant five more miles on the West Fork Dosewallips where our trail joined the main Dose trail at the Forks camp. It was all familiar ground from here, and another five miles put us to the ranger station where we camped in another shelter.

Our luck was with us, for when we arrived at the ranger station we struck up a conversation with a fisherman camped nearby who said he was leaving the next day and if we wanted a ride he was going right by Brinnon and would drop us off there. He was driving an old 1930 Chevy pickup and could only take one of us in the cab, so Ray and I got in the back with all our packs while Bill regaled the fisherman with our harrowing experience in the LaCrosse Basin. The ride was only about 12 miles long, it didn't rain, and we arrived at Brinnon in fine spirits.

So ended our graduation celebration hike. In retrospect it would have been better to have graduated in August.

CHAPTER 6
WEST ANDERSON

As Bob "Pete" Pedersen describes in his section of this book entitled "Mts. Olympus, Tom and Athena," the summer of 1938 was a very busy climbing season for him. He finished off the summer with the following account of a climb of West Anderson with another of our climbing group, Bob Prichard. *(Author's Note: The following account is written by Mr. Pedersen.)*

"By mid-September 1938, an outstanding summer's climbing season was nearing an end. Many of my climbing buddies had returned to school, and I was in the process of packing for a move to Seattle for the start of another college term when I received a call from Bob Prichard asking me to join him this forthcoming weekend for a climb of the West Peak of Mt. Anderson. At the time, Bob was working at the Puget Sound Naval Shipyard, had a car and money enough for travel expenses which was an economic situation neither I nor any of my other climbing friends were in. Bob said he would pick me up after work Friday evening with the plan being to take the Seabeck-Brinnon ferry and pick up some dinner snacks at the Brinnon store to eat en route to the trailhead. We would then hike up the Dosewallips trail until dark Friday night, continue up to the Anderson Glacier Saturday to a climbing camp, then Sunday climb the West Peak. The hike back to the car would be made that afternoon and evening. As they say, this was an offer one couldn't refuse. Not only was the timing right for me, but the plan was excellent, and I would be with an outstanding climbing partner.

We arrived at the trail head as planned, which as I recall was a mile or so above Elkhorn. We were traveling light, taking food for cold meals only, but with a primus stove for hot drinks. We carried sleeping bags, but no shelter and no climbing aids except for 100 feet of manila climbing rope. We expected to make fast time on the trail and probably hiked faster than was necessary. When it became so dark Friday night that we could no longer travel without using flashlights, we bivouacked alongside the trail. This was just short of Big Timber Camp, and we estimated that we would have about 12 miles of trail and 3000 feet of elevation to gain during the next day's hike to Anderson Glacier.

Saturday was a comfortable fall day; the trail was in excellent condition, including the "way trail" to the glacier from Anderson Pass. Camp was made on the moraine alongside the glacier where meltwater was available. Prospects for a successful climb Sunday were excellent. We had about 1100 feet of elevation to gain to reach the top of Flypaper Pass and then about 850-900 feet of rock to climb from the Eel Glacier to the summit of West Peak. As we had both been over Flypaper Pass several times the only new terrain for us would be the summit rock. We got an early start Sunday, Bob carrying his rucksack with our lunch and I the rope. We did not bring ice axes since this was primarily a rock climb and, as both of us were using triconi nailed boots, we did not anticipate any problems on the snow.

We quickly crossed Flypaper Pass, dropping down some 150 feet to the Eel Glacier which we reached about 7:30 a.m. Our route contoured across the upper Eel, passing under Middle Peak (Echo Rock) to the base of the West Peak rock which we started up about 8:00 a.m. The peak resembled a pile of high blocks of rock with broken rock and numerous small ledges. It was class 3 or 4 climbing on which we did not use belays because of the numerous good hand and foot holds and small ledges or benches. The average pitch was probably about 50 degrees although numerous places were 60 degrees with a number of short vertical pitches that could generally be avoided. Our route was as direct as practical. It was enjoyable climbing and, even with several stops for picture taking, we reached the summit about 9:30 a.m., September 17, 1938.

There was a small cairn on the summit covering a pipe tobacco can (Prince Albert or similar) containing a single note. To the best of my recollection, this note was dated about 10 years earlier recording a solo climb by a man who gave an address of either Centralia or Chehalis.He asked that anyone finding the note please contact him.

Unfortunately neither of us made a copy of the note, which I have ever since regretted. In those early days when we were young, few of us thought much about the importance of collecting such information for historical purposes. I believe the guilty feeling I acquired helped to preserve this incident in my memory. *(Author's Note: Those interested in reading the story of 1936 and 1937 climbs of West Peak by Norman Bright - reference Chapter 3 "Camp Cleland" - are referred to his story, "Mountaineering Youth," in the 1943 American Alpine Journal.)*

Bob Prichard near the summit of West Anderson. Echo Rock (Middle Anderson) beyond. Flypaper Pass in far left distance.

Down climbing that rock was slow and disagreeable. After descending some 500 feet, we came upon a narrow, straight snow finger that exited onto the Eel Glacier. It was steep - 55 degrees or more. With about a 10 second discussion, we agreed that we would glissade down to avoid all that down-climbing. I leaped out onto the snow and instantly accelerated. Part way down my feet went out from under me. Rolling onto my stomach, pushing up on hands and toes I regained my feet, only to have the same thing happen a second time. I had just regained my feet this second time when I shot out onto the Eel Glacier. I don't know how long it would have taken us to down-climb that last 300 feet or so of rock, but it felt like nanoseconds. We were pleased, and then I noticed blood running off the tips of the fingers on my hand; a slice from a rock. I still wear the scar - a reminder of that exciting drop.

The descent of Flypaper Pass was simple after that. We made a slow controlled glissade down the upper right snow finger to the rock outcrop midway down, then crossed the outcrop to the left snow field for a fast, safe glissade onto the Anderson Glacier reaching camp by noon. After a 15-16 mile hike on the trail, we reached the car by 6:00 p.m. In no better way could we have capped the end of our summer climbing season."

Mt. Anderson from West Anderson summit. Eel Glacier in foreground, with Flypaper Pass at right.

SECTION II

Dungeness, Quilcene and Tunnel Creek Trails and Peaks (Quadrant 1 Map)

QUADRANT 1 MAP

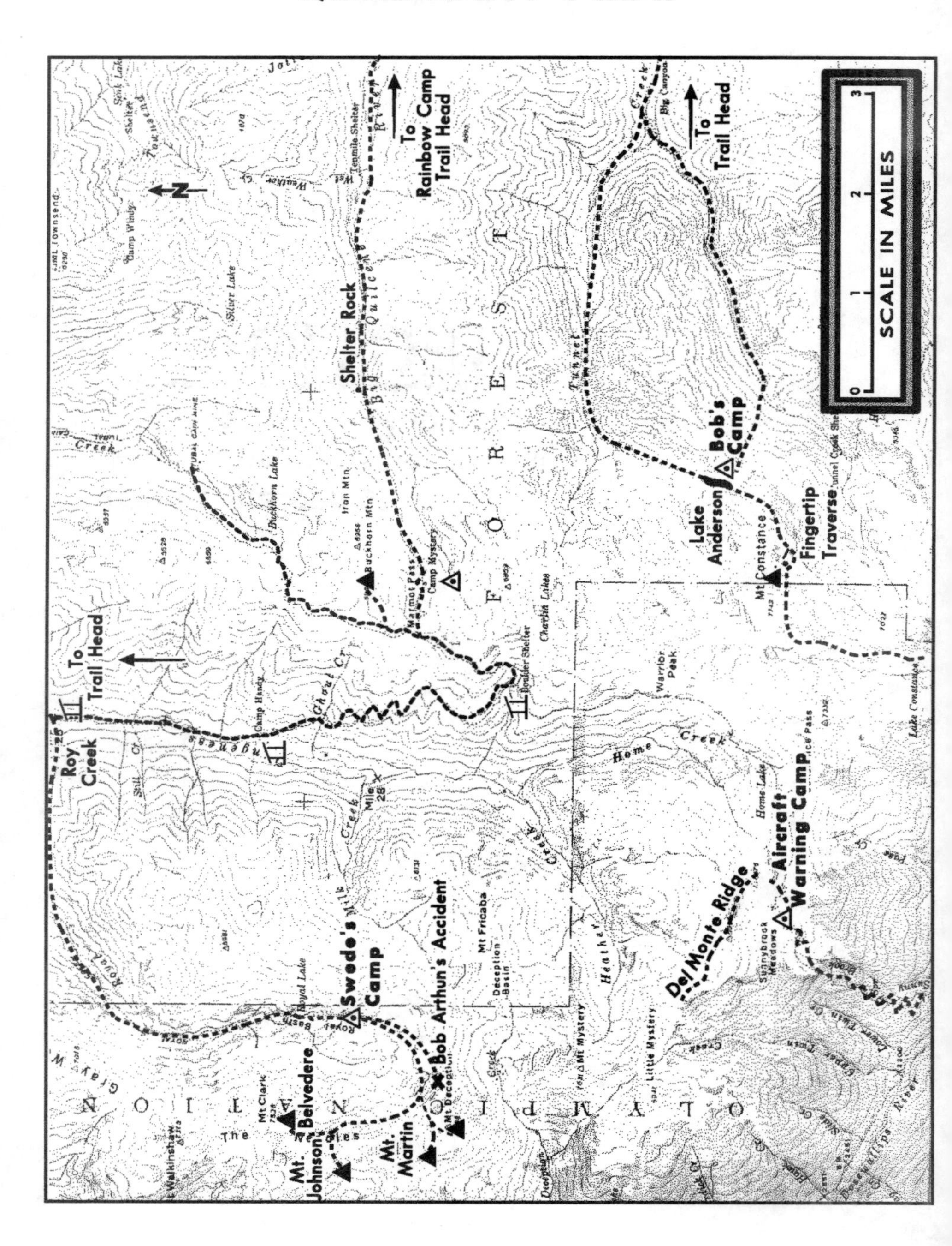

CHAPTER 7
A ROYAL MISHAP

The unfortunate accident we would suffer was not on the agenda when Scout Troop 503 made the customary plans for our July 1936 annual Olympic trek. That would come later. This year we would traverse Marmot Pass, traveling up the Dungeness River, over the pass and down the Big Quilcene River.

As usual, we held a night-before inspection of scouts and equipment at the Bremerton Methodist Church, our meeting place, to eliminate as much as possible the problems that might arise on the trail later. Our leader was Norman Zell, our new scoutmaster, and he had as his assistant the new junior assistant scoutmaster, yours truly. This was a brand new title, and I felt like a real greenhorn. I spent most of the time trying to learn all I could by observing Norm.

After all of the inspections had been made the individual packing began and here was an area where I felt at home as I had been through this annual ritual for the past five years. There was one change that I noted, however. Nearly every scout now had one of the new *Trapper Nelson* pack boards instead of the old homemade "sourdough" boards. This was a vast improvement as it was much easier to pack or unpack, and the improved comfort in carrying the load was phenomenal.

After inspections and packing were completed we were ready, and Norm made the annual announcement: "We leave from in front of the church at 8:00 a.m., so be here at 7:00 a.m. after a good breakfast, and with a brown bag lunch for tomorrow. Go home and sleep well."

Everyone was there, about 20 happy scouts, Norm and I, and we all got into the back of the same flatbed truck I had ridden in on the previous five annual Olympic mountain hikes, and we were off. We again rounded Hood Canal, headed north and, passing Discovery Bay, turned left at Dungeness Bay. Traveling inland on a dirt Forest Service road for several miles, we came at last to the Louella Ranger Station where we got a fire permit for our entire trip. A short distance on up the road we came to the trail head at the Dungeness Forks Camp.

It had been a tough ride in the back of the truck, so everyone unloaded and walked around a little to loosen up, then readjusted packstraps, retied shoes, and we were ready. I was to lead and Norm was to follow as Tail-end Charlie. He cautioned me not to travel any faster than the slowest in the group could manage easily, so I got the smallest scout up front with me and we started out. By making rest stops about every 30 minutes we managed to proceed without incident, paralleling the Dungeness on its east bank through large timber and some underbrush, finally reaching Gold Creek Shelter and our camp site for the first night. We had traveled about four miles from the Dungeness Forks.

Mass transport to Dungeness River.

There was a short break, and then we started putting our camp together. I sort of supervised the erection of all the tents and then Norm and I started dinner. The ranger at the Louella Ranger Station had told us that the trout were really biting and there were a lot of them. Norm suggested to everyone that if they all went out and did a good job of catching fish we might have enough for dinner. The scouts cooperated and proceeded to catch enough to provide a more than adequate meal.

After dinner we built up the campfire and proceeded to enjoy the evening with songs, new stories by Norm, and questions about the day's hike and what to expect tomorrow. The boys were told that we would travel about eight miles to the shelter at Roy Creek where we would camp. Everyone went to bed under a million sparkling stars.

A ROYAL MISHAP

In the morning Norm did the traditional trick and pulled fresh eggs, bacon, and bread and butter out of his pack for breakfast. This was done every year, but after breakfast he reminded everyone that we had just eaten the last of the good stuff. Breakfasts tomorrow and in the future would be rolled oats and dried prunes, with Eagle Brand Milk. (many moans and groans). After we packed up for the day the entire campsite was cleaned up to leave it as good or better than we found it. We then started on up the trail.

Crossing at Gold Creek Camp to the west side of the Dungeness, we started a gradual climb on the west bank of the Dungeness River up through heavy timber but with not too much underbrush. As we got farther up the trail the sidehill became more precipitous. We would occasionally come to a slight break in the trail and could catch a view of the upper Dungeness Valley as well as one to the northeast back down the river to the Forks Camp. After about a three mile climb the trail eventually flattened out and we did some ups and downs. A stream crossed the trail at an appropriate moment, so we had lunch.

Shortly after lunch the trail started dropping and after numerous switchbacks we were again next to the river at River Camp. We continued on up the Dungeness River for another three miles, this time staying next to the river with no major elevation changes until finally we came to Roy Creek Shelter, our camp for the next two days.

It had been a pretty strenuous day, and most of the activities at the camp were limited to preparing a really good camp site for tonight and tomorrow night. One of the patrols was assigned to cooking and pot washing for dinner and tomorrow's breakfast, so their camp life was fixed. The fishing appeared to be pretty fair, too, so we were looking forward to another fish dinner. Norm and I both requested that when a total bag limit of two fish apiece had been caught all others were to be thrown back. This would be about right when added to the rice.

After dinner the campfire was built up and songs and stories occupied the rest of the evening. I announced that anyone wishing to make a side trip up into Royal Basin should see me in the morning and I would lead the group. Then we all went to bed under clear skies again. About seven of us got off to an early start the next morning up into

Royal Basin, the headwaters of Roy Creek. My friend Pete Pedersen led off and I followed. The trail traversed through large timber and roughly followed the creek on its western bank. After three or four miles we started to break out of the heavy forest into some meadows near the creek, interspersed with avalanche-scoured chutes covered with slide alders.

The creek now flattened out and the river bottom was fairly clear of timber. Shortly we came to a steep slope virtually crossing the entire valley, the stream dropping down it in a series of cascades. This was probably an old glacial terminal morain. After climbing this slope we came to beautiful Royal Lake, surrounded by clumps of sub-alpine trees and meadows. From here was a marvelous view on up the valley of several peaks hemming in an extinct glacial cirque, and the beautiful breathtaking ridge of jagged peaks called The Needles.

This seemed like a good place to have lunch, so we lay back in the meadowland and relaxed. We had come a good five miles from camp and I wanted to move on two or three more before returning, so we made a short lunch stop and started on up the valley, passing Shelter Rock, a huge rock overhanging the trail and providing a good place to camp during a storm. After Shelter Rock we skirted a large meadow that I found out later was called Arrowhead Meadow because of its shape. A person could look down and see this from higher in the valley.

Above Arrowhead Meadow the trail climbed up into the cirque, and once again I was fascinated by the beautiful meadows with their multitudinous variety and quantity of wild flowers in bloom. We were startled by the piercing whistle of a marmot, followed by a similar call from the first marmot's buddy some distance away. There were also some deer grazing nearby, completely ignoring us.

Pete wanted to explore the area to the west toward The Needles, so we headed off in that direction under the cliffs of Mt. Deception. There was no trail at this point and we were angling up the scree slope when one of those above must have dislodged a rock that rolled down and struck one of the scouts, Dick Arthun, in the arm. It was a nasty blow and a nasty fall. It was fairly obvious that Dick had a broken arm. He was in considerable pain, and although we had plenty of first aid equipment and knew what to do for a bone fracture we had no medication for the pain. Dick was splinted and his arm strapped to his side and we started down the trail for camp. The jarring as he walked must have been excruciating; we moved very slowly at first. As the retreat continued, however, he picked up speed and was really moving when we got to camp at Roy Creek.

Our annual hike now had a real problem, as Dick certainly couldn't continue but must see a doctor as soon as possible. This presented Norm with a real crisis and as it was too late to do anything until morning I had no idea what was going to happen. I do know that as the leader I was responsible for the accident and felt terrible.

By the next morning Norm had made a decision. He and Pete would escort Dick, with Dick's twin brother Bob, back to the Louella Ranger Station, a distance of about 12 miles, and I would be in charge of the troop for the rest of our annual trek. Once the decision was made things moved quickly. Norm and Pete divided up Dick's pack between them, left most of the food they were carrying with those of us who were continuing, and started back down the trail. Norm had given instructions to the whole troop before leaving that I was in charge. I didn't feel very good about the situation - but the hike was to go on.

We packed up, cleaned camp, and left for our next stop which was at Boulder Camp, a distance of about six miles . It was a beautiful day with a few cumulous clouds and bright sunshine. Today's travel took us for about two miles following the Dungeness River bottom to Camp Handy where we passed some fishermen and two large pack horses grazing in the meadows along the river. The trail passed several hundred feet from where they were, so we didn't stop but walked right on by. A little later it occurred to me that those horses might have expedited Dick's trip to a doctor.

After leaving Camp Handy the trail climbed up the east bank of the Dungeness River, gradually gaining in elevation and leaving the river far below us. It continued in this manner through timber until about half a mile below Boulder Camp when the trees thinned out and frequent meadows appeared. There was a typical three-sided Forest Service shelter here with its open side looking east right up the side of the mountain toward Marmot Pass, our destination tomorrow. (At that time, there were no trees in front of the shelter—just meadows filled with those marvelous flowers and huge boulders scattered helter-skelter all around and up the mountainside. Mature trees completely surround the shelter today).

In my present leadership capacity I had a great fear that some new calamity might befall us. As the safe continuation of the hike was on my shoulders I had the urge to forbid anyone to leave camp. On the other hand these guys were basically responsible and they had signed up for the hike, and I knew that they would be very careful, particularly after Dick's experience. As there were no fish in the little trickle of water adjacent to camp, exploring in the immediate area was the main activity. The huge boulders were stacked up in such a random fashion that large caves and crevices had been formed and were just asking to be explored. My only instructions were to stay with your buddy and be careful. All went well although I didn't enjoy that day very much. The only real excitement was watching a black bear a couple of hundred yards up the mountain roam around the meadow digging and scratching for food. The campfire that night was a bust although everyone tried to be happy. They all missed Norm and the rest of the fellows.

Next morning brought another perfect day. After breakfast and camp cleanup we packed and started up the trail for Marmot Pass and Camp Mystery just beyond it. We would travel only about a mile and a half to the pass, but with a gain of about a thousand feet in elevation in the process—not far, but a lot of work, nevertheless.

We took it slowly and in a little over an hour had reached Marmot Pass. The trail started up in timber, then gradually changed to subalpine and then to alpine country with all those great meadows. The marmots were signalling back and forth to each other on all sides. It was quite a serenade.

Shortly we were at the pass, and what a view! To the west could be seen Mt. Fricaba, Mt. Deception and The Needles - all of the peaks that we had seen rimming Royal Basin just two days before, and to the left was Constance Pass and beyond it Mt. Mystery and Little Mystery. The sky was now cloudless, the day was warm, and we were n another Olympics Heaven.

About half a mile through the pass we came to Camp Mystery, a good spot situated in a grove of alpine firs. It was still mid-morning and we had the whole day ahead of us, so I suggested and everyone agreed that we should climb Mt. Buckhorn. This peak was right above us to the north and was 7000 feet high, probably higher that most of us had ever climbed before. We unloaded our packs, I issued our rye-crisp lunches and we started for the summit.

We retraced our steps to Marmot Pass, then turned north, then east on the slopes of Mt. Buckhorn. It was an easy scramble, quite safe, and we were on top by a little after noon. It was a marvelous view in all directions, and Mt. Constance, south of us, appeared to be quite close and not a whole lot higher. The only drawback to our climb was the lack of water. It was a bare dry mountain and we knew we had to go clear back almost to Camp Mystery to quench our thirst. So we did. The rest of the day was spent making a good two-night camp and then exploring the immediate area. We expected to be cold that night, and we were. There was no wind though, and if a person put on all the clothes he had before climbing into his sleeping bag he would be fairly comfortable.

I had suggested just prior to bedtime that we take another side trip the next day and visit the abandoned Tubal Cain Mine. This was met with enthusiasm so the next morning following breakfast, after issuing rye-crisp biscuits and requesting that all those who had canteens fill and bring them, we started again back to Marmot Pass. At the pass we turned north again, following the ridge that led around to the west of Mt. Buckhorn, climbing slightly with the ridge, then descending and turning east, switchbacking down alpine meadows to Copper Creek and finally to Tubal Cain Mine.

There wasn't a whole lot to see, as the mine itself was boarded up and the camp was pretty much a wreck, but at least we could say we had been to Tubal Cain mine.

On approaching camp we noticed smoke, and wondered if we had visitors. Sure enough, we did. There was Norm, Pete, Bob Arthun and Mr. Mill, one of the troop committeemen. When everyone recognized who the newcomers were there was a noisy celebration. Norm and his party were greeted as if they had returned after a lifelong absence. Shortly things quieted down a bit and Norm got to tell us what had transpired after his party had left us at Roy Creek. They apparently got to the Dungeness Forks where there was a field phone and called the ranger at the Louella Ranger Station about four o'clock. The ranger placed a call to Dick's parents and made arrangements for the Brinnon-Seabeck ferry to hold and then drove Norm's party to the ferry landing in Brinnon. Dick's parents were waiting in Seabeck and drove everyone into Bremerton. Dick had his arm set late that day. After a night's sleep Norm and his party left for the mountains again, this time for the Rainbow trail on the Big Quilcene River, spending the night at the Ten Mile shelter. The next day (today) they came on up to Camp Mystery for our reunion.

It was a great weight off my shoulders to have Norm back and in charge, although I had absorbed a lot that I would be able to use on future hikes. It was with relief that I learned that Dick was OK with no serious problems. I still had that feeling of responsibility that wouldn't go away. I was learning a mountain lesson that one wouldn't normally find on an ordinary trail hike—such as when off the trail look out for rolling rocks, and never let the party get one person directly above another.

The next morning we packed up and had an uneventful hike through big timber down the Big Quilcene River, passing Shelter Rock Camp (no relation to the camp in Royal Basin) and on to Bark Shanty Camp for the night. The next day we climbed up out of the Rainbow Canyon to Rainbow Camp on the Olympic Highway.

There we were met by parents and friends and best of all with Dick, complete with arm cast, for the annual "welcome back" picnic at the trailhead (including potato salad) and the end of an interesting if different trek.

CHAPTER 8
THE NEEDLES

The group of spires making up The Needles is one of the most challenging in the entire Olympic Range. Climbing in The Needles was pioneered by Swede Johnson and George Martin and is related by Swede in these climbs.

By Elvin R. "Swede" Johnson

"George," I called down in guarded delight. "There isn't a Boy Scout in sight and not even a cairn." As George Martin joined me on the rocky summit, we searched for any trace of a previous visit. There was none. "Well, Swede," George said with his hearty booming laugh. "I think we have a first ascent."

Our climb that late July day of 1940 was a prominent rocky peak about a mile north of Mt. Deception. It was the southernmost high summit of the rugged pocket range known as "The Needles." The actual climb preceding the above conversation is described later and dubbed "Martin Peak."

George and I, together with two other Bremerton companions, Wesley Wager and Jim Swanson, had taken a week off to explore this seldom visited beauty spot of a rugged section of the Olympic mountains. The peaks, composed of jointed basalt, rose prominently between the upper valleys of the Dungeness and Gray Wolf rivers. We had seen these exciting serrated pinnacles from the summits of several mountains, including the constance group. It had, however, taken us a couple of years to find the time to enter the area. One can now drive almost to the National Park Boundary near Roy Creek camp, but in pre-war years it was a long approach with the trailhead starting at Dungeness Forks, the confluence of the Gray Wolf and Dungeness Rivers. A backpack of 15 long miles was required before the base camp area was reached, nine of them up the Dungeness to Roy Creek and then another steeper six up a poorly maintained trail into Royal Basin. This consumed the better part of two days with an overnight at a campsite at Roy Creek. We established our permanent camp near a huge basaltic boulder called Shelter Rock, in the flower-strewn meadows of Royal Basin with its small glacial lake. To the north, the west and the south loomed the jagged peaks that had lured us there.

The Needles seen from the east.

On that day, our first full one, all four of us had accomplished the ascent of Mt. Deception, which at 7,788 feet elevation was the second-highest peak in the Olympics behind the west and middle summits of Mt. Olympus. The weather was ideal and as dawn broke, we left camp. We scrambled up into the divide between Deception and one of our later objectives. It was a long ascent, but not a difficult one. We did not even uncoil the rope.

We reached the summit and thoroughly enjoyed the panorama of great Northwest scenery. The view was not confined to the snow, rock, glaciers and greenery of the Olympic mountains. Hood Canal and other waters of Puget Sound lay below us, and above the summer haze, distant peaks of the Cascades were in evidence, including the great bulk of Rainier. On that day, however, we were more intrigued by the sight of the dark, serrated peaks of The Needles range just to the north, whose summits seemed only slightly lower than Mt. Deception. As the hour was still before noon, one of us suggested trying the nearer Needle that afternoon. The idea was quickly agreed upon, so we descended back into the saddle between Mt. Deception and nearer peak.

Mt. Deception was the only climb on which Jim and Wes accompanied us as they both enjoyed scrambles through the meadows and over the lower ridges instead, with a little fishing added. There they left us, while George and I began to work our way up the ridge through a veritable maze of steep rock gullies, short chimneys and ledges. We encountered a great number of unstable rocks and, as a result, we stayed close together so that no dislodged pieces could do any damage. We frequently had to leave the jagged ridge for the more feasible chimneys and ledges east of the ridge. Later, Jim and Wes told us that they could partially follow our progress by the occasional sound of falling rock.

The route finding problems were many, but we always seemed to find a way up. We actually encountered few difficulties with only a few class 3 pitches and virtually no exposure. As a result, we approached the summit fully expecting it to be festooned with Boy Scout banners. It was not, however, and we had a first ascent of the 7,550 foot peak, although it had not been a climb to excite the great mountaineers of the Northwest.

George carried a heavy monstrosity of a camera with him on most climbs - a huge folding Graflex. It was big and cumbersome, but it surely took some magnificent photos. While photographing, I heard him say to me, "Swede, for the records I suppose we had better give this a name." I recall replying, "George, I have already named it Martin Peak. After all, you are the senior member of this party." He laughed in his resonating voice and said, "I don't really believe that I could get by at the high school if anyone found out that I had named a peak after myself."

I urged him to accept it for a couple of weeks until we settled on a name to turn in to *The Mountaineers*. He was still laughing at the idea as we began the descent to our camp far below.

The weather remained clear and beautiful, and the next day our objective was another and apparently higher peak to the north of "George's Mountain," as I now called it. We left camp early following a good breakfast and trudged up into the lower part of Surprise Glacier over the terminal moraine to a spot almost east of our new summit. Here, we studied the rocks and decided to angle up and a bit to the south and attempt to get to the ridge between Martin Peak and our objective. With some careful route finding up chimneys and gullies along some ledges, we topped the rugged ridge in about two hours from our stop in Surprise Basin.

There, we began to have doubts as to the wisdom of having chosen this route. The ridge above not only appeared to be steep, but it was festooned with sharp pinnacles and nasty-looking narrow little chimneys. It was too late to fret about it, so I led off to the first obstacle. As we scrambled up, we encountered several difficult pitches where we used the rope occasionally for safety. As we encountered a short steep pitch, George called up with a chuckle, "Remember, Swede, I have a wife and two children that I'm responsible for." I replied, "I'll try not to kick a rock on your head, George." (Helmets were not yet used.)

At several difficult spots, we swung over to the west and were soon able to reach the base of the summit block. There we chose a chimney of about class 4 and perhaps 100 vertical feet. By the rock climbing standards of today, the chimney was no great feat, but over 50 years ago, it was a bit of a struggle. However, following 20 or 30 minutes of stemming, huffing and puffing and clutching basaltic handholds, we stood on another previously unclimbed summit. This one was obviously the highest in The Needles, at 7,650 feet.

Joyous congratulations were in order as George said, "Well, Swede, Mt. Johnson is a pretty impressive peak." I laughed and replied, "Okay, it's Mt. Johnson for a couple of weeks, but we should name both peaks after your wife and daughters."

"That would spoil them, Swede," he said.

We decided to try to descend directly down into Surprise Basin. With only limited rope, we reached the basin in perhaps two hours or less. As I recall, Wes even greeted us at camp with a few scrawny eastern brook trout to garnish our basic macaroni supper.

We realized that we only had another day or two at the most, but George and I had one more objective and perhaps two before departing on the long hike out. The foremost focus for the next day was another jagged basaltic peak with two or three summits. It was located to the east of Surprise Basin, and it appeared that it might present some difficulties. We carried a few pitons, but I do not recall having to use any as our rope slings sufficed for belays and rappel points.

So, that early morning we plodded back up across the terminal moraine into Surprise Basin, but this time, we continued onto the col at the head of the basin at about 6,500 feet. There we paused for a mid-morning snack and studied the possible routes while enjoying the unfolding panorama of rugged snow and rock peaks catching the light of the sun as they rose above still shadowed glacier-carved valleys.

We debated the possibility of traversing all the way around to the north ridge or face, but it was a long way and an unknown quantity when we arrived. We, therefore, agreed on a very feasible appearing broad, but steeply sloping ledge whose lower steps could be reached by perhaps 200 vertical feet of broken and jointed, but fairly sound rock. The ledge sloped back to the south and appeared to terminate at the base of steeper, but still deeply shadowed chimneys into which we really could not see.

George Martin on one of The Needles pinnacles.

Some joyable class 3 scrambling brought us to the lower reaches of our ledge. Its three or four hundred feet of length offered no great difficulties. At that point, we moved up into the broad chimney with a large room-size boulder in its lower reaches. We bypassed it with only scrambling and moved above it another one or two hundred feet to where we discovered the chimney divided. At that juncture, the right branch appeared to be the more feasible approach to the ridge south of the summit. We remained roped and used caution up this class 3 chimney to avoid many loose rocks. Reaching the ridge crest, we discovered that the remainder of the ascent took on the appearance of a steep broken south face rather than that of a ridge. It looked pretty imposing, but by this time we were becoming quite excited. I believe I remember telling George that perhaps he should forget his wife and two children for the next hour or so. I think he ignored my facetious remarks as we moved up to the nearer chimneys, which were much narrower and steeper than the larger one which brought us to the crest.

It was always a puzzle to know just which chimney to take, but, in general, we stayed in a direct line to where we thought the summit to be. An hour or so of good class 4 climbing with several belays, but no great exposure, brought us to the short summit block. There we again anticipated total success, but we didn't know what we would find on that ultimate pinnacle. The steep final pitch up a deep crack brought us to the long-awaited and airy summit. It was a repeat of the previous two endeavors. No one had been there before. We build our cairn and left our register, but decided not to name the peak until later.

Why, I do not remember, but the strange fact is that we did not give it a name until I had returned from the Italian campaign with the Tenth Mountain Infantry Division. There in the Appenine mountains of Italy, guarding the Po Valley, was a heavily German-fortified mountain named Monte Belvedere. In a concentrated early morning attach, it was finally taken, but with great loss of life to our outfit, the 86th Mountain Infantry Regiment. So, we finally named our first ascent "Mt. Belvedere" and the name surprisingly remained until about 1970, when it was officially renamed "Mt. Clark," honoring Irving M. Clark, a prominent conservationist. Thus ended our highly successful assault in the summer of 1940 of The Needles.

CHAPTER 9
BOB'S TALES

Bob Prichard was one of the prominent members of our informal hiking and climbing club. He started his journeys to the Olympics very early, and I felt it appropriate that he should relate some of these, if for no other reason than to get a different perspective of how things were in the early days. After some persuasion, including help from his wife, Alda, he agreed. In his words, "I have searched my memory bank and will relate, somewhat sketchily I must admit - because of memory drain - a few of my outstanding trips."

By R.G.Prichard

ELWHA AND HAYES RIVER

My first venture into the Olympics was in May, 1931 when I and two of my apprentice colleagues from the Puget Sound Naval Shipyard packed up the Elwha River as far as the Hayes River where we made a base camp at the shelter built by the Forest Service. Our first camp was below the Elwha Dam and that evening we got into conversation with a packer named Joe Stanley who owned a place in the area. He mentioned that his pack string was soft from a winter layoff and for a fee of $15 each he would pack us in as far as the trail was open. We took him up on the offer and next morning set out with one pack horse and our own mounts.

On the trail past Whiskey Bend we saw an old shack with a crudely written sign on it "beer, wine and hair-cutting." The trail was in terrible condition with lots of deadfalls that we were able to get over or around and we managed to progress as far as Elkhorn shelter before we were stymied by some large trees over the trail. At that point we felt we had gotten our money's worth, for at that time Elkhorn was about 15 miles in. Joe turned around and headed out while we set up camp for the night.

The next morning Fred and I discovered to our chagrin that our turning over of the menu-planning to Guy, and the purchase thereof, was a terrible mistake for he had purchased canned stuff galore - even stewed tomatoes and salmon. We divied up our load and set out with our extra heavy packs for the seven mile trek to the Hayes River. To this day I don't know how we did it with those heavy packs and having to clamber over and around so much debris in the trail.

Just before we got to Hayes River, in trying to crawl over a log, my pack overbalanced and I went over the log head first with my pack pinning me down. I did manage to extricate myself and we made it to base camp. We spent a couple of days based there, climbed Mt. Claywood one day and dinked around on the river the next without catching any fish. The next day, in making up our packs, we discovered we had brought in about twice as much food as we needed. I had to pull Fred off Guy he was so mad about the waste of our hard-earned money, for we were each making $13.90 a week at that time. We left a well-stocked shelter with our canned food and headed out, camping that night at Lillian creek and out the next day. That was the one and only time we teamed up together.

HAMMA HAMMA VALLEY

Over the next few years I made numerous trips into the mountains - once with a mixed group of four couples up to Upper Lake Lena. This was in the mid-thirties and, at that time, they had just pulled up the logging train tracks up the Wacketikeh (now the Hamma Hamma) road, and you had to walk over an old logging trestle that was pretty high. The road had not been cut in at that time to the present trail head where the Tumwater Scout Council had a camp at Lower Lake Lena called Camp Cleland. It was *real adventure* camping for the kids, and most of their supplies were packed in by mules.

In the mid-forties, the council voted to close down Camp Cleland and build a more civilized camp at Summit Lake. This would enable the scout leaders to take their rocking chairs to camp. Today, not a trace remains of Camp Cleland. Even the Forest Service shelter which was further down the lake is totally gone. The fishermen and campers having taken a few shakes at a time off it for their fires. The same fate has befallen most of the Forest Service built shelters.

A few years later I decided to try another cross-country climb from the Hamma Hamma road up to a saddle in the Baldy (now Lena) Ridge. According to my topography map, if we headed due west straight up the hill, we could come in northeast of Mt. Stone and above Scout Lake which is usually reached by coming in past Upper Lake Lena. Two of us couples packed a lunch and decided to make a day hike of it and see if it would be feasible to later make it a pack trip.

Several miles past the Lake Lena trailhead we turned off to the northwest along a logging road spur and drove along it for a considerable distance to its end where we parked the car. From there we hiked on in a westerly direction, crossing Boulder Creek and heading directly up Baldy Ridge. When we topped out we were in a small saddle near a small pond. The route did indeed seem doable. Alda and I planned on a backpacking hike up this route and to camp on the ridge for a couple of days.

While at the store buying grub we ran into John Morgan, director of the Tacoma YMCA . We suggested that he, his wife and son, Jay, accompany us which they agreed to do. This time we had packs, and it turned into a strenuous undertaking. We are still friends of the Morgans, but that turned out to be a real test of friendship. We did eventually win the saddle and had beautiful weather and two moonlit nights where we could see the panorama of lights all around Puget Sound. In the daytime I looked down on Hood Canal and even made out Case Inlet where our home is located. It was well worth all the hard work, but I would not recommend it for the fainthearted. It has been many years since then, and the logging road has since been absorbed by nature.

FLAPJACK LAKES

Another trip I recall was up to Flapjack Lakes with my two

younger brothers. I had just purchased a new pair of boots and had what they called *sliver hobs* put in the soles. This made for a pretty heavy boot, but I felt I could go anywhere in them in perfect safety. I did some pretty harebrained stuff in my younger years: this trip was no exception. At the top of Gladys Divide there is a long snow finger to the east that goes up to a saddle. I wanted to go up there in the worst way. I had no ice axe, so I just cut myself a stick, left my brothers at the bottom and set out in my invincible boots to climb the finger.

I kicked steps all the way up and finally achieved the saddle where I had a wonderful view of Hood Canal. Way off to the east I could make out the Smith Tower in Seattle which at that time was the tallest building west of the Mississippi. At my feet lay beautiful Mildred Lakes. Having taken in the view, I started down, very carefully planting my feet in the steps I had made on the way up. All of a sudden the snow broke out under my *invincible* bootsI lost my stick and began the slide of my life down that finger, trailing my hands behind me for steering and dropping my heels from time to time trying to slow my speed. My two brothers saw me come rocketing out of that finger in a cloud of snow, and I stopped short of where they were with a very sore pair of hands and feeling pretty foolish. The very next week another guy did the same stunt, but he wasn't as lucky - he crashed into the rocks and was hauled out with a broken leg. I guess I had a guardian angel, and his wasn't paying attention.

The Bremerton Ski Cruisers - summit of Mt. Constance.

MT. CONSTANCE

In 1938, after a very traumatic divorce and in an attempt to quell the constant ache in my insides, I tried playing golf. It didn't help very much, but I somehow managed to make contact with the Bremerton Ski Cruisers which at the time was mostly a hiking and climbing group. They had a climb scheduled for Mt. Constance, so I decided to go. I think I still had my invincible boots, but no other climbing gear. There were 11 of us in the party, six girls and five guys. Paul Crews was leading the group, and I think this was our first meeting. For the life of me, I can't remember the names of the guys or some of the girls so I won't try to name them except that my future wife, Alda was there.

The climb from the trail head to Lake Constance is a real killer. It's mostly a two mile scramble, but once at the lake it becomes worth all the effort. You can't see Mt. Constance from the lake and you need to know the route. Paul had been briefed on it, so he led the way up a long valley almost to the end of it when he cut to the right up a long steep snow finger. On the way up the valley we were kept under surveillance by a big old mountain goat who watched us all the way up to the finger. We had a 120-foot length of rope and one ice axe. I believe Paul had a pair of boots with *triconi* nails, I in my *invincibles* and the rest in a variety of boots and clothing that would fall far short of today's standards.

Lake Constance.

We did attain the top of the finger by climbing up the length of the anchored rope, each person coming up hand over hand. By repeating this process we attained the top of the finger and our first view of Mt. Constance. It still looked a long way off. We had a sloping shelf of rock to go along that looked pretty hairy. To play it safe, we played out our rope for a safety line and soon all of us were across the traverse. There was hardly room on the summit for all of us, but Paul did find a place to stand on his head, which I learned was a ritual he performed on his other climbs.

We made our descent without incident, going across the traverse and down the snow finger using the same techniques we used on the way up. Our group later got together at the Bremerton YMCA where Ome Daiber, a well-known Seattle mountaineer, gave us of tips on climbing techniques that later proved invaluable.

Another great trip I made with my scout troop was a climb of Mt. Constance coming in from the northeast side. We were curious about how accurate the topography map was, so we started up the Tunnel Creek trail which heads near Quilcene. Where Tunnel Creek forks, we left the trail and followed the right hand fork that, according to our map, followed a valley that would lead us up to where we could approach the mountain from the east side. It was amazing how accurate the elevation lines checked out on our map, for it had been made many years before when they didn't have the sophisticated techniques which later developed. We camped at a small lake that didn't appear on our map. There was no sign of anyone having camped there before us. We named it Lake Anderson after Tony who swam across it and back. He was our only scout who could brave the chill of that cold mountain lake. We decided that it was a fine place to make our base camp. The next day we resumed our climb without packs, and I was amazed to discover that we came in at the top of the saddle I described in my earlier climb with the Bremerton Ski Cruisers. We negotiated the same traverse I had experienced before and all made the scramble to the top of Mt. Constance.

We made an uneventful return to our base camp and next morning, after consulting our map, decided to head toward the east fork of Tunnel Creek in order to intercept the trail and avoid having to beat the brush we had encountered on our way in. It looked feasible on our topography map, and we made it without encountering any unmarked cliffs.

SECTION III

East of the North Fork Skokomish River (Quadrant 2 Map)

QUADRANT 2 MAP

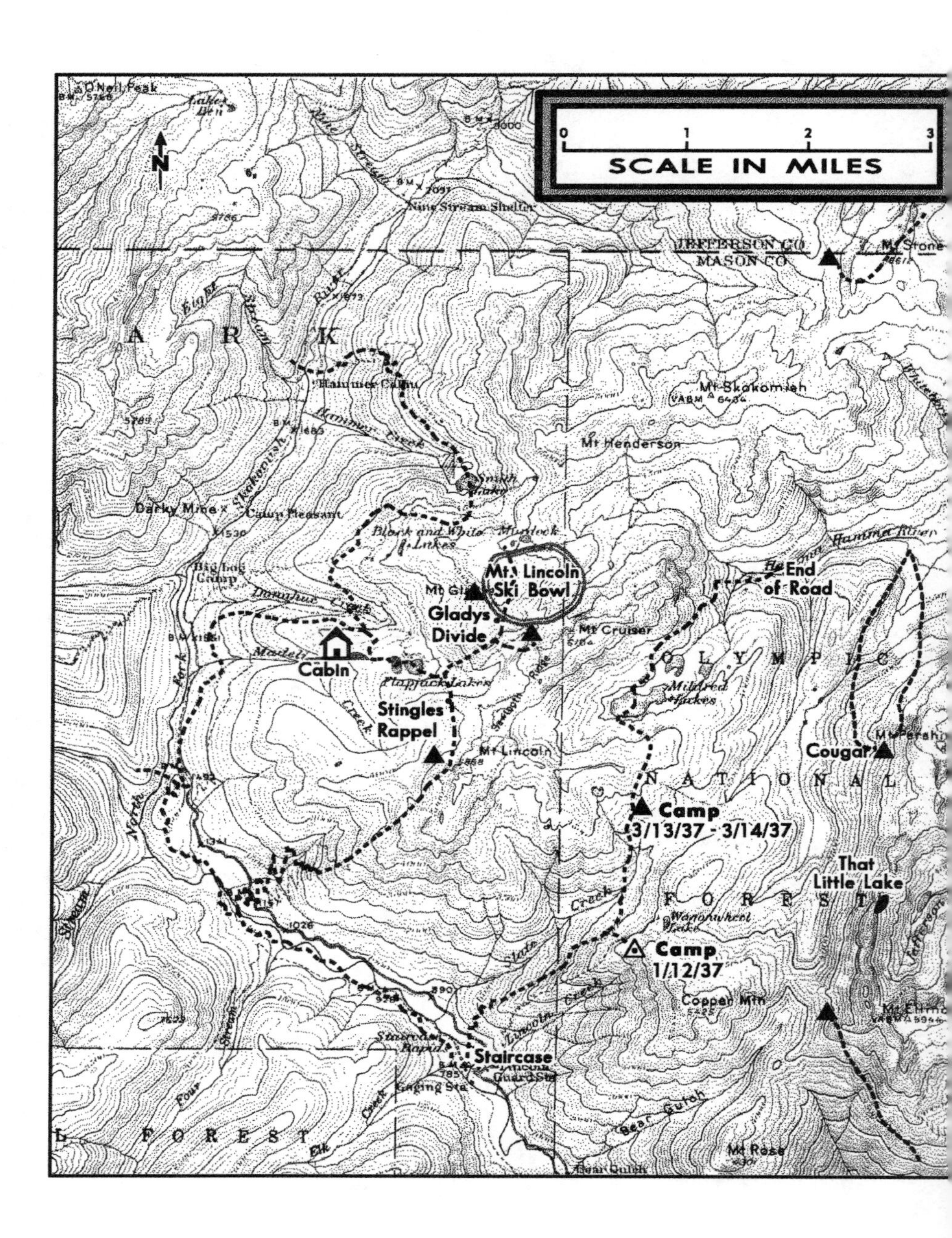

CHAPTER 10
FLAPJACK LAKES

One of my favorite areas in the southeast Olympics is Flapjack Lakes, the other adjacent lakes and Sawtooth Ridge. This area was initially explored by the military party led by Lt. O'Neil in 1890, but his efforts were primarily directed toward travel up the north fork of the Skokomish River, and very little exploration was conducted on its southernmost tributaries.

There was additional activity in this area, however, from a group of five who prospected, staked their respective claims and mined at Black and White Lakes beginning about 1907. Rumor has it that the name was coined by the packer who brought them supplies. A portion of the load was always Black and White brand Scotch whiskey. Remnants of their cabin still remain at the lakes.

It would appear that there were two trails constructed as access to the mines: one partly on the ridge north of Donahue Creek, extending from what is now Big Log Camp on the Skokomish River to Black and White Lakes, a distance of about 2 1/2 miles. The other trail extended from the vicinity of Eight Mile Creek and Hammer Creek on the Skokomish River trail, east on the north side of Hammer Creek, turning south then west above Smith Lake, and terminating at Black and White Lakes, a distance of about three miles. This latter trail has long since been abandoned although a portion of it is still used on the trail from Black and White Lakes to Smith Lake.

As a historical note, a miner named Hamer made his claim in 1909 at the junction of the Skokomish River and one of its tributaries. The tributary was later named for him, but over time spelling has changed to Hammer. He continued to work his claim and trap until 1920 when he died alone in his cabin of natural causes. He and the miners at Black and White Lakes must certainly have socialized and worked together to some extent (B & W Scotch?), otherwise, why would there have been a trail connecting their claims?

A couple of other miners, the Smith brothers, had a claim near Gladys Divide about 1914, and Smith Lake was probably named for them, as their claim was nearby. They later prospected further up the Skokomish, and may have had some interest in the trail from the Hamer claim to Black and White mine.

Black & White Lake.

Poor old Frank Donahue, another early miner, spent many years prospecting the North Fork Skokomish River, but never found anything, leaving nothing behind but his name on a creek.

Black and White Lakes, Flapjack Lakes, and Smith Lake are all concentrated in a small area on the western slopes of Mt. Gladys, all connected by less than three miles of trail. Murdock Lakes, about one mile northwest of Gladys Divide, is not connected by trail, but easily accessible over meadows and snow fields. They are about 2 1/2 miles from Flapjack Lakes, only one mile of this not on an established trail. This, then, is the greater Flapjack Lakes area, bounded on the west by the Skokomish River valley and on the east by the spectacular group of spires called the Sawtooth Ridge, with Mt. Lincoln on its southern end and Mt. Cruiser the anchor on its northern end. It is probably the most popular hike-in site in the Olympics.

A third trail to Flapjack Lakes was later constructed, probably by the Forest Service, from the Skokomish River road about four miles north of the Staircase Ranger Station, at a much gentler grade. The Forest Service road formerly was open even beyond this trailhead, but in later years was closed above Staircase.

One of my earliest memories of the area was during a day hike my father and I made to Black & White Lakes in late summer. We hiked in on the Forest Service trail, later descending by the steeper trail on the north bank of Donahue Creek. The blueberries were in prime condition when we got to the lakes, and we proceeded to demolish a few hundred of them. I recall sitting down in one place, and without moving filling my alpine hat to the brim with berries. Needless to say my mother was delighted to get the hatfull of berries, and also ecstatic over the new blue tinge to my britches.

On another trip a few years ago my son, David, and I were making a traverse of the ridge between Mt. Gladys and Mt. Henderson, and while en route passed the two small Murdock Lakes in a beautiful alpine valley of meadows and alpine fir groves. There were elk tracks and droppings everywhere, and we were disappointed at not seeing them. Later, while hiking along the ridge and unable to find a suitable campsite there we elected to drop down to the West to Smith Lake.

Murdock Lakes.

Just as we left the ridge, we saw a herd of at least 50 elk laying down on a snow field below. We were able to get to within about 50 yards before they stood up and left us, running through meadows and snow fields until out of sight.

It was getting dark, and we were about half way down to the lake through meadows and slide alder when we crossed the abandoned trail between Black and White Lakes and Hammer Creek on the Skokomish River trail. It was flat, there was water nearby, and so we camped. We were practically overpowered by mosquitoes before we got the tent up and crawled inside for the night to escape the rascals, but we slept well and were bugless the next morning.

Instead of following the half-obliterated trail over to Black and White Lakes, we followed our original plan and dropped on down to Smith Lake. It was a beautiful day even though the sun could not overcome the shadow caused by the Mt. Gladys-Mt. Henderson ridge. The fish didn't seem to mind, however. They were feeding on insects on the lake's surface, and there seemed to be plenty of them. This must be a favorite site for fishermen, as we noted at least one raft secured to the bank although we found no fishermen.

The trail up from Smith Lake to the Black and White Lakes trail was extremely steep, but short, and we continued our retreat uneventfully to Staircase and then home.

About 1934, a bunch of us started making hikes to some of the more interesting areas of the Olympics, and Flapjack Lakes were included. We were really impressed with the beauty of the region, particularly by the spectacular Sawtooth Ridge. Mt. Lincoln I remember caught our attention since in those days there was a trail part way to the summit. A forest fire in 1985 swept the area, destroying the trail.

Swede Johnson, Karl Stingl and I made this climb in 1936 and, while we were having lunch on the summit, enjoyed the seldom seen view to the east. There were the remote Mildred Lakes nestled in a tributary valley of the Hamma Hamma River, as well as the outstanding sight of the western side of Mountains Ellinor, Washington, Pershing and Jefferson, the backside of the coastal range seen from points east of Hood Canal.

Swede thought it would be a good idea to return to our car by descending into the Flapjack Lakes Valley, and led off dropping down and skirting the west side of the Sawtooth Ridge until we were above the valley.

Smith Lake.

At this point we reached an impasse, and Swede elected to rappel down an extremely steep gully to a point where we could continue our descent to the lakes. We only had 100 feet of rope, but that would be adequate to reach the bottom if not doubled. Swede dropped on the 100 foot single line, reaching a point about half way down that would serve as an anchor for a doubled rope for the rest of the rappel.

Upon hearing this shouted word from Swede, I proceeded to retrieve the single rope and double it for our rappel. I then instructed Karl in rappeling technique as he had never done this before. Karl at that time was a brand new immigrant from the Sudetenland in Czechoslovakia, and his English was very elementary, but quite understandable: "I don't go down that damn hole!"

It took much urging from me and shouts from Swede below to convince Karl that it was either that or return over the top of Mt. Lincoln. He finally accepted his fate, and carefully, but slowly descended to where Swede was waiting. We continued rappeling to the bottom of the gully, at which point Karl stated with great relief, "I don't never do it again" and to the best of my knowledge he never has. On the other hand he was a Class A ski jumper, only about 16 years old, jumping over 60 meters at that time. My personal comment would be "I don't jump off that damn thing" if I were at the top of the jump in-run.

Many of the adjacent pinnacles in the Sawtooth Ridge were climbed by members of our summer hiking and climbing club at about this time, but as no cairns were left or reports documented, first ascents have been credited to others.

Flapjack Lakes.

CHAPTER 11
THE CABIN

Skiing was a rapidly expanding winter sport in 1936. A few months after our Lake Lena ski initiation over New Year's 1935-36 (see chapter 15 "To Ski"), a new outing club in Bremerton, the Bremerton Ski Cruisers was formed, and its elected officers were anxious to locate a new ski area close by. These officers were: President, Al Couch; Vice President, yours truly and Secretary, Virgina Laing. Board members were C.J.Ritchie, Mr. Searcy and Mrs. Morse.

The search for a ski area in the Olympics that would be convenient to Bremerton was conducted by the club in the winter and spring of 1937. C.J.Ritchie, one of the founders and leaders of the brand new Ski Cruisers, made a chartered air search and came back with excellent photographs of a large open area that seemed ideal for our purposes. Unfortunately, there were insufficient landmarks to positively identify its location, and C.J. thought it was on the east side

First Exploratory Party - January 1-2, 1937.
On the trail to Wagonwheel Lake.

of the Sawtooth Ridge adjacent to Mt. Lincoln. Our new illusive area was, therefore, dubbed the "Mt.Lincoln Ski Bowl," and a search by foot was next on the agenda. Our first abortive winter expedition was made on skis by George Martin, Bob Scott, Pete Pedersen, Chuck Thompson, Bob Brotherton, Jack Kirk, Ray Layton and me. Our destination was Wagon Wheel Lake and beyond, a climb above the Staircase road for about three miles and a gain of 3,000 feet elevation. This trip was for three days over New Year's 1936-37.

We all had climbers for our skis, but the trail was very steep with lots of switchbacks; and our backpacks, complete with winter camping gear, didn't make things easier. We ended up breaking trail through a foot of snow, carrying our skis, and finally reaching Wagon Wheel Lake at dusk, very tired and wet with a cold night awaiting. Needless to say, it was a new experience for all of us. After floundering around for most of the next day - January 2, 1937 - trying to reach the top of the ridge above the lake, we gave up and returned to camp and home the next day.

On March 13-14, 1937 the second search for the Mt.Lincoln Ski Bowl took place. It again started up Wagonwheel Lake trail - why, I can't remember because it led us east of Sawtooth Ridge. Most of the hikers and climbers in the group, after reviewing aerial photos again, felt that it was west of the ridge based on their summer trips to Flapjack Lakes. In any event, the party consisted of C.J. Ritchie, Bob Scott, Guy Madden, Chuck Thompson, myself, a young skier from Hoodsport named Lee Dickinson, and one other unidentified member from an old photo.

This was much better organized than the previous search. We now had compacted snow on which to ski, the temperature was quite mild, and we had had a couple of months to improve our skiing technique. Our route followed up Slate Creek, contouring around from Wagon Wheel Lake, then over the pass between Slate Creek and a Hamma Hamma tributary. We camped for the night on that stream and early the next morning skied down the fairly open slopes to Mildred Lakes. From this point on my recollection of the trip is of a complete disaster. I know that we skied down the outlet of Mildred Lakes, sliding down gullies, walking logs across canyons (carrying skis), climbing over and under logs, finally reaching the end of the Hamma Hamma logging road just as it was getting dark.

Mildred Lakes.

A dinner had been planned in Hoodsport to celebrate our reaching the Mt. Lincoln Ski Bowl (which of course hadn't occurred), but plans were progressing for the evening and, sure enough, cars arrived to pick us up within about an hour of the time we reached the road. We were met in Hoodsport by members of the Hoodsport Chamber of Commerce and by Bremerton Ski Cruiser members who had driven down from Bremerton for the event. We were all dead tired, but C.J. Ritchie made a speech extolling the wonders of the Mildred Lakes area, and nearly everyone attending was satisfied. Most of us searchers fell asleep at the dinner table. So ended the second search for the Mt. Lincoln Ski Bowl.

As mentioned previously, some of us who had been active in the Flapjacks Lake valley really believed that the Mt. Lincoln Ski Bowl was near Mt. Gladys. So, on April 17-18, 1937 Chuck Thompson organized a group of 21 members of not only the Bremerton Ski Cruisers, but also members of the Shelton Ridge Runners to hike up to Flapjack Lakes while snow was on the ground to confirm our belief that this was the actual location of the Mt.Lincoln Ski Bowl.When the party arrived at the lakes it found six or seven feet of snow on the ground, and thethreesided Forest Service shelter half-full of snow. Apparently it was an exciting night, as all 21 people crowded into the small cleared area within the shelter. It was reported that no one slept very much.

Second Exploration Party March 13-14, 1937. At Slate Creek Divide. (Mildred Lakes in the distance.)

The next day the party skied on up to Gladys Divide and, lo and behold, they were greeted by a beautiful ski area consisting of open slopes interspersed with groups of alpine firs - wonderful ski country. It was at least two miles from Mt.Lincoln, but completely covering Mt.Gladys' north and east slopes. It extended east to the Sawtooth Ridge and down the meadows of the southwest tributary of the Hamma Hamma River below the slopes of Mt. Henderson.The bowl exceeded our greatest expectations, for the slopes of Mt. Gladys were excellent with varying degrees of fall and ski-able almost everywhere. The best part was that it was only four miles from the end of the road to Flapjack Lakes and another mile-and-a-half to Gladys Divide. Man, had we wasted a lot of energy on the first two searches, and all in the wrong place!

The summer and fall of 1938 were filled with activity. The Shelton Ridge Runners were asked to participate in the construction and ownership of the ski cabin at Flapjack Lakes, and the two groups proceeded immediately to get the project underway. This construction was all hand labor, utilizing seven-foot cross-cut saws, axes and frows to make shakes from cedar logs. Two loggers from Shelton were hired to do most of the construction, with volunteers from both clubs providing grunt work on week-ends and vacations. Trees and downed logs were cut up, and the walls, joists and rafters were hand-hewn, all from local materials. Flooring, nails and similar materials were brought in the four miles from the trailhead by a hired packer with horses. I believe even the stove was carried in. It was well into the fall when it was completed, and we had a big cabin-warming to celebrate the completion.

Despite the satisfactory construction of the cabin in 1938, there was still a lot of effort required to keep things going.

The following rules were established by the two clubs:

HOUSE RULES FOR CHALET

• *No drinking in chalet* • *Have two leaders in chalet each week*
• *Each member pays before going to chalet*
• *Rates for 3 meals and 1 night lodging: club members $1.25 club guests $1.75*
• *Safety rules - no smoking on second floor*
• *Skiing parties must consist of not less than three members at one time*
• *Never wander off alone*

Immediately following completion of the cabin and having suffered the torture of the four mile trail to Flapjack Lakes, some of the Ski Cruiser members proposed initiating an effort to get the road extended to the lakes. Our summer climbing and hiking club was unanimous in being against this, but the winter-only skiing group really pushed the idea. C.J. Ritchie contacted the Forest Service to pursue the idea of having the CCC build the road, and was informed that the Forest Service would be unable to make more expenditures in the area.

This attitude, I believe, was because of the change in status of the Mt. Olympus National Monument to the Olympic National Park in this same year. There was a major effort by the conservationists at this time to increase the size of the park, taking additional lands from the Olympic National Forest. Sure enough, it happened in 1939, and the area west of the ridge dividing the Skokomish drainage from the Hamma

The Cabin.

Hamma drainage became part of the Olympic National Park. The drainage east of the dividing ridge remained in the National Forest, but became the Mt. Skokomish Wilderness. This development brought on a serious concern to the Ski Cruisers as, although the exact location of the new boundary was not precisely delineated, the probability that Flapjack Lakes were now in the park was real.

Ski Cruiser club minutes note that at the April 12, 1939 meeting the club received news that the Mt. Gladys ski bowl might be taken into the park. Also, on October 11, 1939 it was decided to spend no more money on the Flapjack Lakes cabin for building material and other expenses until the ownership status was clarified. The concern was that the Olympic National Park would assume ownership of the cabin. The club basically felt that it had put a great deal of effort into the cabin at this point It was a valuable asset and should be retained if at all possible.

Prior to December 1939 the cabin was infrequently locked, and maintenance fees were supposed to be (but seldom) collected by those using the cabin. Because of the change in land status, legal brains in the club suggested that no fees be charged and that use of the cabin would be for members or guests only. This was apparently to forestall claims by outside parties that it was a public facility. A new lock was installed.

In April 1941 a special use permit was issued by the National Park Service to the Bremerton Ski Cruisers and the Shelton Ridge Runners for an annual fee of $17.50 plus insurance.

Although the whole idea of the ski cabin and ski bowl had been a major project of the Ski Cruisers, it was apparent that many of the members preferred driving to Mt. Rainier for the skiing area and housing facilities it offered. I must admit I was one of this group. Club minutes reflect this trend, also that nearly all maintenance was done by the hiking and climbing club.

This maintenance was actually performed by Art and Viola Landry with the help of several scouts with whom Art was associated. Some of the maintenance they accomplished included replacing the ridge pole that had been destroyed by a falling tree and cutting up a cedar log over a mile away for material to make the necessary replacement shakes for the roof. They also sawed up another downed tree that blocked access to the cabin for use as firewood. These were major projects, but they also provided many more mundane services such as cleaning up garbage brought in by others and relocating the full outhouse. No credit was ever given to Art and Viola for these good deeds, and I hope this late acknowledgement will help to replace the oversight.

The vast majority of the Ski Cruiser members never visited the cabin and this resulted in very few winter trips to the Gladys Ski Bowl, nearly all of these by members of our hiking and climbing group.

One of these winter trips over Christmas 1941 will always stay in my memory. I know that there were seven or eight of us, including Swede Johnson and Bob Prichard, possibly Chuck Thompson and two or three others whose names I can't recall. We hiked in the four miles, skiing the last two after finding considerably more snow than expected. Upon arrival at the cabin we were presented with the necessity of digging down through about four feet of snow to the door. Unfortunately the cabin shovel was inside, so we improvised using skis and obtained entrance after only about 30 minutes, with a broad stairway packed into the snow.

We had arrived in the late afternoon and continued to carry out housewarming activities including starting a fire in the wood stove, breaking a trail to the lake and opening a water hole. It didn't take long for the cabin to warm up, and while we were arguing over who would cook dinner we heard a rustling in the wood pile and our first thought was ***rats***. Nearly everyone grabbed a ski pole, and we were just about to start dismantling the wood pile when out crawled a tiny Civit cat!

Everyone immediately backed away, and the kitty walked around the cabin as if it owned the place (it actually did at that point). It apparently was unafraid of us and behaved like a good little cat. We finally figured it would be good if we respected its presence, so dinner was started in a very cautious manner and by the end of the evening everyone was used to the situation. We all decided to sleep on the second floor loft, as the Civit cat apparently had no interest there, preferring its wood pile home.

In the morning we were up with the sun, and as soon as the cabin had warmed up again out came kitty. Bob Prichard mixed a little

Eagle Brand milk with water, placing it in a tin plate on the floor. When we left for a day of skiing on Mt. Gladys the cat was busy licking up the milk. That night, the same thing happened. As soon as the stove heated up the cabin our little friend again came out of the wood pile. Bob offered it more milk again, and it lapped it right up.

Now Swede is a very nervous guy, and he had been fretting about the skunk's presence from the very first. He finally said "This is ridiculous. It's our cabin and the cat must go!" He proceeded to locate a wooden bench adjacent to the door, put a fresh pan of milk on the floor at the end of the bench, and put on his right ski mitt. Then he climbed on the bench on his hands and knees. The cat was still licking up the milk with its tail erect. At this point Swede instructed us to open the outside door, which was done, and after holding his right arm up in the air, started a long straight-armed sweep out, down, and toward kitty. Using extraordinary control he grabbed the cat's tail midway of his swing and then, following through, released his grip and it flew out the door and up the steps, alighting about 10 feet away. The door was instantly closed, and we all breathed a sigh of relief. Unfortunately, we also breathed the aroma rising from Swede's ski mitt, and it was immediately condemned to the outdoors.

We were all commending Swede on his excellent solution to a perplexing problem when we again heard rustling in the wood pile, and - you guessed it - kitty was back! It showed no animosity toward us and went over to the milk pan to finish its meal. Needless to say, we were all super cautious from that point on and really kept an eye on Swede to keep him under control. Two more days of skiing was enjoyed, and then we said goodbye to kitty and left for work or school, realizing it had been a marvelous holiday, albeit somewhat exciting.

It was February 1946, about five years later, and my wife Betty and I were staying with friends at their Skykomish River cabin and skiing every day at Stevens Pass. In those days there were three rope tows in a row just above the lodge carrying skiers up the mountain one tow after another. I had just arrived at the top of the lower tow when I spotted Karl Stingl. I hadn't seen him since before the war, and we talked for awhile. I asked if he had seen Swede. Karl replied "Ja, he iss here somewhere." We said goodbye, and I kept my eyes open for him. Suddenly I caught the unforgettable aroma of skunk. Turning around, I saw Swede about 10 feet away, holding out a very smelly mitt. Because of old times' sake I stuck mine out, too, and with a handshake we greeted each other for the first time in almost four years. If it had been anyone else but Swede I wouldn't have touched that mitt with a 10 foot pole.

With the advent of World War II, a majority of the climbing group was off to war, and those remaining were too few to maintain the cabin. The National Park Service, some time after 1948, reclaimed the cabin and removed it and the old Forest Service shelter.

Today, I am sad to say that Flapjacks Lakes will probably never be returned to the wonderful place it once was. There has been a significant loss of the wilderness atmosphere in later years, even though the Park Service has put much effort into trying to preserve it. It is just too popular and the hands (and footsteps) of man are too much to overcome. On the other hand, I'm optimistic for the future of the rest of the Olympic National Park. Major trails are in acceptable condition with no appreciable overcrowding and the new generation of hikers and campers is doing an excellent job of hauling out its garbage, leaving campsites spotless. The lesser trails and off-the-trail areas are still uncrowded, and I am enjoying them as much as I did 60 years ago.

Epilogue: The Bremerton Ski Cruisers still exists as a very successful club. In 1947, the membership started work on a new lodge at the Stevens Pass Ski Area, completed it in 1948 or 1949 and are now enjoying it to its fullest. Even then there was better skiing and lodging less than three hours driving time from Bremerton, when compared with a minimum of five hours travel to Flapjack Lakes, including a four mile hike. In retrospect, it was a much better area in which to build than Flapjack Lakes. Our near-sighted efforts in 1937 were wasted except for the camaraderie and cohesive purpose of the small group responsible for the completion of the club's first cabin. Many of these same people were involved with the second cabin as well.

Although Mt. Rainier and Stevens Pass - actually the entire Cascade Mountain Range - hold a charm that is outstanding, I'll always remember fondly the many hours we spent at Flapjack Lakes.

CHAPTER 12
MT. CRUISER

I had held Mt. Cruiser in awe since the first time I saw it. There it was, a freestanding stone finger, rising several hundred feet from its base, with no obvious way for a person to climb it.

As early as 1934 a group of us from high school saw the Sawtooth Ridge for the first time and became fascinated with it. At that time we were breaking away from scouting activities and trying climbs of greater difficulty. I was an avid reader of stories about pioneer climbers, most of them about the Alps: Whymper on the Matterhorn and Mummery and his pioneering of unguided first ascents. Closer to home were the tales of the Pacific Northwest. These were Mt. Rainier - *A Record of Exploration* by Meany; *Our Greatest Mountain* by Schmoe and *Snow Sentinals of the Pacific Northwest* by Hazard. I also found *The Conquest of Mt. McKinley* by Belmore Browne. All of them seemed to say that the ultimate satisfaction is in choosing your own route and following it to the summit.

We had timidly made ascents of Mt. Gladys and a couple of lower points (then unnamed) in the Sawtooth Ridge and were eager to follow in the footsteps of Whymper and Mummery, so were climbing more and more difficult peaks. We were really in awe of the impressive and unclimbed peak at the north end of the ridge, the highest in the whole group.

In the fall of 1937 a party of the Bremerton Ski Cruisers made an overnight outing to Flapjack Lakes and a visit to the proposed ski area around Mt. Gladys. Three of us, Ray Layton, Harry Winsor and I had discussed earlier the possibility of climbing this highest needle in the Sawtooth Ridge. This trip seemed the ideal time. The peak was immediately adjacent to the Gladys Divide, the weather calm and clear - in fact a beautiful day, as delightful fall colors were beginning to show at this higher elevation.

The three of us left the others in the party and kicked our way up a snow finger that terminated in a notch in the ridge. We had all been this far on an earlier exploratory trip, so knew the route well up to the final assault. We turned left (north) at the notch, dropping down and following under the ridge until we came to a steep gully that led up to huge stacked up rocks, car size or larger that we were able to climb under and over, thus allowing us to reach the base of the needle itself.

At this point Harry, an excellent amateur photographer, elected to sit on top of the adjacent ridge and watch our progress. Ray and I examined the peak and made our way out on its south face on a sort of ledge or crack between a flake of rock and the main peak. Ray set up a belay and I led off for the summit about 70 feet higher. We estimated the face to be at about a 70 to 75 degree pitch, and I was able to find finger and toe holds (though hard to locate) and proceeded slowly. In those days we had no pitons or other aid other than the climbing rope, and I was extremely cautious. Occasionally I would reach an impasse, but Ray, from his location, would call out suggestions of possible holds that proved doable.

About 10 or 15 feet below the summit, I reached a point on the southwest knife edge that provided a resting place and belaying point. After a short break I belayed, and Ray came on up. From this point it

Mt. Cruiser.

was a short scramble to the top, and we both felt as if we had conquered the world. From the summit we could see Harry, and the rest of our party at Gladys Divide, and immediately realized that they were having lunch and that we were starved and thirsty. We waved, they waved and shouted, and after a short rest we started down.

Upon reaching the belay point we secured our 100 foot climbing rope over a rock outcrop and Ray rappeled the 60+ feet to the ledge above the flake. This left me with a problem, as our 100 feet of rope was not adequate for me to rappel on a doubled line clear to the ledge. I didn't want to rappel on a single line, as this particular rope was a brand new manila 4-strand climbing rope, and I couldn't afford to abandon it.

I contemplated the situation for awhile, then asked Ray how solidly he was set on the ledge. He said he was in good shape, so I explained what I was going to do: rappel as far as I could on the doubled rope, then continue down until I held the extreme ends of the rope, one in each hand. This would put me to a point where Ray could almost reach my feet. I would then let loose of one of the ends, hold on to the other end, and with the help of rope friction around the rappel point and friction between my body and the rock, Ray could grab and hold me. We proceeded to carry out this procedure. Ray's grip of steel when I got within range was very comforting, believe me!

Harry came down to join us with our lunch, and we had a celebration picnic on the spot. We discussed all aspects of the climb, and Harry asked numerous questions about certain points in the climb that I couldn't even remember. One item I do recall: from his nonpartisan position Harry stated that we should always carry extra ropes. He was right. I had come to the same conclusion, and in retrospect had decided that I should have abandoned the rope and returned later to retrieve it.

In any event, our reconstruction of the climb finally ended with the trickle of water below Gladys Divide beckoning us. We cautiously descended the snow finger, quenched our thirst and rehashed the climb with the rest of our party at the divide. I suggested that the peak had earned a name. The Bremerton Ski Cruisers had contributed to its first ascent, and we should name it "CRUISER."

And so we did.

CHAPTER 13
MT. PERSHING

One of the few members of our climbing group that ever bothered to keep records of his exploits was Don Dooley. The following account describes the first ascent of Mt. Pershing, the "lonesome peak" in the heart of the Hamma Hamma River valley completely surrounded by Hamma Hamma tributaries.

By Don Dooley

Early in the week of August 20, 1939, a friend of mine, Lieutenant (JG) John Speer called: "Don, I have a weekend free. How about if we do a climb? I thought it would be great to do another like last month when we did Rainier with Pete Pedersen and Bob Prichard." I was pleased because Johnny's first climb ever was less than a year ago when we completed the second ascent of Mt. Cruiser with Swede Johnson. (My friend Paul Crews and Ray Layton made the first ascent the year before). I suggested, "How about Mt. Pershing? I don't think anyone in the Bremerton area has ever done it, so it may be interesting."

Viewed from the Puget Sound area, Mt. Pershing is inconspicuous, but can still be seen with other Olympic peaks on the horizon. It lies between Mt. Washington and Mt. Stone. Nevertheless, when identifying Mt. Pershing, The Brothers to the right is more distinguishable than Mt. Stone from a distance. During the First World War local residents named it in honor of General John "Black Jack" Pershing, Commander of United States troops in Europe at that time. George Martin, the founder of the Olympic College Mountaineering organization and co-author of the illustrated map of The Olympic Peaks, later noted, "From certain points, a profile appears which could resemble the General. The name first appeared on forest maps in 1920."

Friday night Johnny called to say he had duty as officer-of-the-day that coming weekend, but could his friend Lieutenant Mandelhorn,

U.S.N. go in his place? So early on August 27 saw Bob Mandelhorn, Walt Ingalls, Bob Henderson and I, members of the climbing club of the Bremerton Ski Cruisers, on our way. I remember vividly; it was a bright, vibrant, and sunny sunday in late August 1939 - not a cloud in the sky - as we drove around Hood Canal to the Hamma Hamma River.

After driving to the end of the road and parking, we could look up the steep north side to what appeared to be the summit of Mt. Pershing and decided to go around the west side. We shouldered our packs and started up the short trail that took us into the basin between Mildred Lakes and Mt. Pershing. Although it was only about a mile long, it was a poor apology for a trail. Evidently it hadn't been used for years.

We were aware that the basin, or perhaps valley would be a better description, was extremely remote and seldom, if ever, frequented in the thirties. This hidden valley went south for several miles at an elevation of three thousand to thirty-five hundred feet. It was heavily forested and had no access trails except this short one from the Hamma Hamma road which was not maintained. (Today the trail has been extended to Mildred Lakes below Mt. Cruiser). The valley is surrounded by the jagged Sawtooth Range on the West, Copper Mountain and Mt. Ellinor on the south, and Mt. Washington and Mt. Pershing on the east.

As we progressed up the valley a deathly stillness permeated the dense forest. Suddenly we heard the sharp snapping of branches in the underbrush. Quickly we turned to see a black hairy creature bounding away through the brush and over logs. Someone cried, "It's a bear!~Look! There's another!" The second black bear leaped after the first; both were hell-bent to escape from the intruders.

We climbed out of the valley in a southeasterly direction until we reached a long scree slide on the west slope of Mt. Pershing. Struggling to gain elevation in the sliding scree, we approached the cliffs above. About a hundred feet or less below the rock face, I looked up in an effort to scout the best way. I couldn't believe my eyes!

I yelled, "Hey, look! Isn't that a cougar?" There at the top of the scree slope below the first cliff was a large tawny mountain lion. He was nervously pacing back and forth unable to go up and unwilling to go down toward us. There was no hesitation on our part; we quickly angled to the right giving the big cat plenty of room to maneuver!

We carefully worked our way up a large gully and chimney system in the west face until we reached what we thought was the top. As we stood on the summit and glanced around, it was evident this was only the middle peak of a large massive jumble of three peaks. The southernmost was a few hundred feet higher so we hauled our packs onto our shoulders and headed southeast down to the saddle between both summits. After a scramble from the saddle, we finally reached the highest point. To our amazement there was no register, cairn, or any other sign of a previous party. We had no idea until that moment that this was a probable first ascent. Stop to think of it, I had heard no one mention the mountain. This indeed was a primitive part of the Olympics.

As we dug into our packs for a late lunch, we gazed out across Jefferson Creek valley to nearby Mt. Washington and Mt. Ellinor. Large snowfields hung in the shadows of the very precipitous northwest face of Mt. Washington directly across from us. The needle-like Sawtooths culminating in the Mt. Cruiser spire rose above Mildred Lakes against the western sky. To the north lay Mt. Stone across the Hamma Hamma River valley and, farther to the right, lay the dominant Brothers with Mt. Constance beyond.

Another arm of the extensive Mt. Pershing massif angled out to the northeast and contained several small summits. The highest one, near the end is a few hundred feet lower than Mt. Pershing's highest. It was later climbed for the first time in 1958 and named Thorson Peak by Keith Spencer and party, although locally it was called Mt. Jefferson.

Directly east was an unparalleled panorama on this exceptionally clear and sunny day. Below sprawled the blue of Hood Canal. Beyond, the Puget Sound area was dwarfed by the distant snow-covered Cascades and the white glaciers of Mt. Rainier.

When we arrived back at the middle peak, I got the bright idea that it would be shorter to go directly down the north side to our cars and perhaps find drinking water. "Besides, we can avoid all that bushwacking," I reasoned. So we scurried north along the ridge and over the lower north peak - still no sign of a previous ascent. We apparently could claim first ascents of all three peaks! Then the fun began! We roped up and down-climbed the first steep section directly below the north peak. A small stream to our right ran out of a shallow basin and down the north side. It was obviously a more gradual route although we could not see what lay beyond the basin where the stream dropped out of sight. So we unroped, and followed the stream.

Mt. Pershing. Sawtooth Ridge. Mt. Lincoln Ski Bowl in the distance.

In those days few bothered to carry water because of the many mountain streams. We stopped to quench our thirst with pure water from the cold mountain stream. It had been a long dry spell climbing on the west side and summit area without water. When the small basin finally disappeared onto the steeper slope below, we discovered a serious miscalculation had been made. Soon we were down-climbing over slippery moss-covered slabs in the stream bed; rappeling over waterfalls as the gorge became narrower and steeper; hanging on to slide alder and fighting our way through vine maple and devil club. The late afternoon sun had dropped below the ridge on our left and a breeze began to blow down the stream bed from the snow fields above. It chilled our bodies when it came in contact with our wet clothes. Finally we reached an easier, more gradual area just before stepping out onto the Hamma Hamma road —civilization at last!

I look back today with smiles of nostalgia on this marvelous encounter with a wilderness area of long ago. Yet I am sad with the knowledge that the area will never return to the pristine virgin wilderness of those bygone days.

CHAPTER 14
THE CLUB

The participants in the episodes contained in this book were members of our "Club", and almost all of them either grew up together in Bremerton or moved there early in life. This was never a formal club. We had no officers, kept no minutes, and as a result no records except early photo albums, news clips, and just plain memories. They all had a common bond, love of the mountains. Although many of the club's activities included hikes and climbs in the Cascade Mountains, with ascents of all of the major volcanic peaks, the major interest was in the Olympics. The group's formation evolved from early childhood interests to adult recreation, with more participants joining as the years went by. Some of the activities date back to the early 1930's, and there are a few of us still around who get together and reminisce these activities and still make hiking or skiing trips together.

The start in climbing and hiking for most of us, however, goes back to our early scouting days about 1930 when we attended summer sessions at Camp Parsons, the Boy Scout camp on Hood Canal, as well as extended scout troop hikes in the Olympic mountains. As we grew older our interests matured, and scouting began to take a back seat to other high school activities. Our scoutmaster, Gordie Hudson, was a great leader and exponent of hiking and must take credit for our continuing interest in the Olympics. There came a time, though, when he felt that we should make room for younger boys, so he very diplomatically moved us out of the troop and into the Masonic youth Order of De Molay. It wasn't very long after joining the De Molay that we also became members of the "outside" order of the Rainbow. (The "inside" order of the Rainbow was another Masonic affiliate of girls about our age). We would have our "outside" meeting in the school yard across the street from the Masonic Temple. We all brought wood for a campfire, but when the "inside" order closed their meeting and the girls came down the steps of the Temple we would put out the fire and then escort the girls home. A few members of the "inside " order later became members too. This group of former scouts was the nucleus that started our hiking and climbing club. The club became larger as more guys with similar interests in the mountains joined us. As I recall, our loosely-knit group began with Bob "Pete" Pedersen, Jack Kirk, Bob Brotherton, Chuck and Jack Thompson, their cousins Loren and Dick Thompson, and myself. It later expanded to include Harry Winsor, Carl Rusher, Ray Layton, Bill Eldridge, Bob Scott, George Martin, Jim Swanson, Bob Prichard, Art Landry, Bob Henderson, and others still later. Members of the High School Ski Team joined us, including Bob "Swede" Johnson, Don Dooley, Karl Stingl and Jim Pappas. George Martin, Bob Scott and Jim Swanson were around 10 years older than us and a stabilizing influence.

About this time skiing became popular, causing the formation of the Bremerton Ski Cruisers, an outdoors activities organization which we all immediately joined. The Bremerton Ski Cruisers was founded in 1936 and we subsequently carried out summer outings for the ski club, including long week-end hiking and climbing trips, and obtained many new candidates for our club from the skiers, including wives, girl friends and other single girls of about our generation.

The female contingent, to the best of my memory, consisted of Lois Euler, Viola Johnson, Alda Jones, Leona Smith, Toni Soyat, Billie Cooley, Ruth Carlow, and others whose names escape me. As could be expected, a number of romances blossomed between members. Viola married Art Landry, Ruth married Bob Henderson, Alda married Bob Prichard, Leona maried Pete Pedersen, and I'm sure others. Two of these, Bob Prichard and Pete Pedersen are authors of two of the included climbs, as well as one by Swede Johnson who married later to another lady hiker and skier. All three have had long, happy marriages. It must be because of a common love for those high alpine meadows!

Many hikes and climbs were carried out up until the outbreak of World War II, and a few are related herein. Those members living in Bremerton continued their mountaineering activities, but were restricted by gasoline rationing. After the war most of us were gone, and while a few of us would occasionally get together it was far from the Olympic Mountains and was mostly talks of previous hikes. The enclosed tales relate experiences enjoyed by members of our original group with the exception of the chapter entitled "The First Years" which describes how I personally became "hooked" on the Olympics.

SECTION IV

North of the Hamma
Hamma River
(Quadrant 3 Map)

QUADRANT 3 MAP

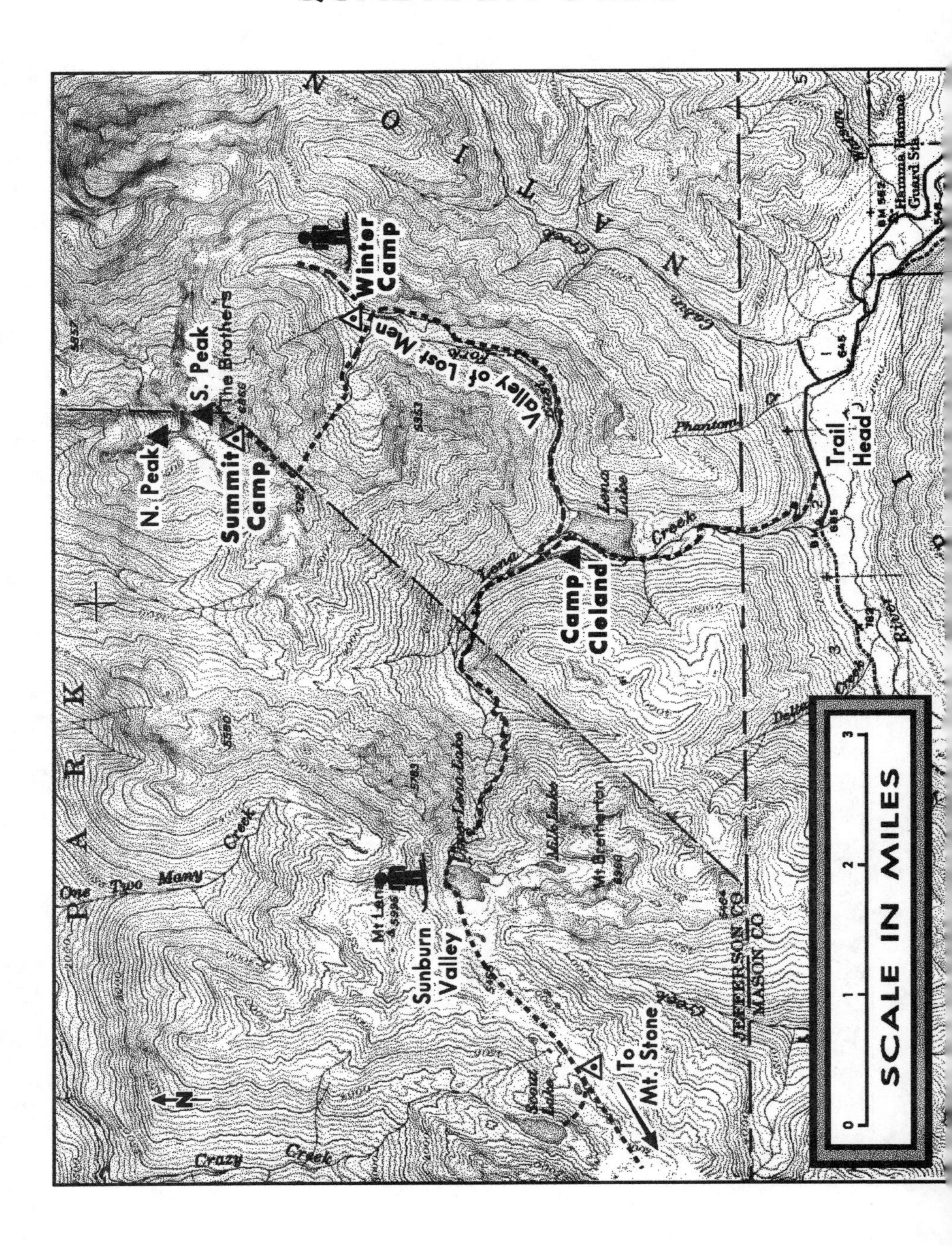

CHAPTER 15
TO SKI

The annual long mandatory wait between October and the following June to further pursue our Olympic adventures was a frustrating situation that Pete Pedersen and I decided to change. Among all of our hiking friends we were the most serious and enthusiastic about winter camping and hiking, and had been the leaders in pursuing these activities in the early thirties, all of it in the back country of Kitsap County. This had been in a locale with no snow cover and temperatures usually above freezing. We decided if we were to expand our activities in the Olympics we must equip ourselves for snow travel.

We had sent for plans for home-made snowshoes from *Boys' Life,* the national magazine published by the Boy Scouts of America, and followed the instructions as nearly as we could. One problem was obtaining hickory for the frames. None was available so we substituted oak, and after trimming to size and shape proceeded to steam and bend the frames to a form we had manufactured. The plans called for using a steam box, but we had none and decided to substitute. Our high school physics teacher had explained that boiling water was the same temperature as the steam it gave off if they were both at the same pressure. We figured boiling would have to do, so rigged up a 10 foot length of two-inch pipe, plugged at one end, and leaned it over a fence at about 45 degrees with the open end up. After filling the pipe with water we built a fire under it. With one frame in the pipe the water was boiled for about 15 minutes. We then placed our frame in the form and left it for 24 hours. This was followed by the second one, etc. There were four frames, so it took awhile.

They turned out beautifully, but there was no snow available on which to use them. Mine ended up hanging on my room wall although I believe Pete actually did use his.

Shortly after the snowshoe project in early October, before we had an opportunity to try them out, we had a major change in plans. On one of our regular Friday night trips to the Rialto theater Pete and I and some other friends saw a black and white short film entitled "The Ski Chase", with good guys and bad guys racing over the snow, and traveling tremendous distances in hardly any time at all. As far as Pete and I were concerned this beat the heck out of snowshoeing.

This was in the fall of 1935, and we started immediately planning for a ski trip that would let us enjoy the Olympics in the winter as much as summer. Our goal was to make this trip on the three-day holiday over New Year's 1935-1936, and we put together a party of the two of us plus Jack Kirk, Bob Brotherton and Adelbert Fesler. None of us had ever skied before, and we all anticipated a marvelous time.

Getting skis and equipment was the first problem, but our difficulty was solved through our old friend the Sears Roebuck catalog. We had a selection, and I settled on a pair of seven-foot ash flattop skis, with no metal edges of course and a mortise (slot) through the mid-point of the ski through which a strap was passed, then buckled over the boot toe. Illustrations in the catalog, however, indicated this method of securing the foot to the ski was obsolete, and that new fangled "bindings" were the thing. These consisted of steel toepieces that could be adjusted to fit the shape of the toe of your boot, with side plates on each side to keep the boot in line with the ski. Slots in the side pieces allowed a toe strap to hold the boot on the ski, and a leather heal strap with a metal tightener to keep the shoe pushed into the binding.

The last piece of equipment required was a pair of bamboo poles, about 48 inches long, with leather loops at the top for wrists and rings at the bottom to give a bearing surface against the snow. As I recall, our approximate expenditure was: skis $7.50, bindings $1.50, and poles $1.00. All we had to do was plug the mortise slot with a piece of wood and screw on the bindings. The bindings adjusted very well to our eight-inch high hiking boots, so we were ready.

I had obtained a copy of Arnold Lunn's *Alpine Ski-ing At All Heights and Seasons* and it was avidly read by all of us, although all it described was snow conditions at different times of the year - nothing on technique. One of the others, Jack Kirk I believe, located The

Mountaineers December, 1930 publication that actually described, with illustrations, the various turns.

New Year's day 1936 was a Wednesday, and we planned to leave the preceding Monday night and be gone on Tuesday, Wednesday and Thursday, returning home Thursday night, January second. We were right on schedule, and hiked in to Camp Cleland on Lower Lake Lena on Friday night and laid out our sleeping bags in what must have been a wood shed. We had been lucky, so far,as there was no snow on the ground and the temperature stayed at just below freezing.

The next morning we were up early and left our camp and packs for Upper Lake Lena, but carrying our skis, poles and lunch. We could hardly wait to get to the snow and try out our new equipment. The first two miles was a bare trail, and then the work began.

The "skiers" at Upper Lake Lena.

This is the point where the trail starts up, and it does so very abruptly. We continued on for about another mile, in snow now, and when it got about six inches deep we decided to put on skis and utilize our new-found aids to climbing in the winter. Anyone who has ever done any skiing knows that the first day (sometimes the first season) is a disaster. None of us had ever been on skis and we were all falling down, not able to make any progress at all. This was very frustrating, so we reverted to carrying the skis, finally reaching the lake about noon, thoroughly exhausted, soaking wet from perspiration, but in beautiful terrain and 18 inches of snow.

Our trail had climbed over the small ridge at the eastern side of the lake, and there was a gentle slope from here down to the lake. We sat down on our skis, eating lunch and resting, trying to decide how we were going to proceed in view of our lack of success on skis earlier in the day. We were all beginning to get cold because of our wet clothing, so Pete and I decided to try that gentle slope, doing exactly what The Mountaineers article had described. We took off, went about 50 feet straight down the fall line in soft, dry snow and simultaneously fell down when we came to a slight rise in the slope. After getting up we walked around on skis for awhile, then side stepped up the slope to our point of beginning.

By that time we were warm again, and were discovering that side stepping was fairly easy, particularly if you were in someone else's tracks. We tried the slope again, this time taking the dip with one ski a foot ahead of the other for balance, and we succeeded in going another 100 feet before falling again.

The other fellows thought that if we could do it, so could they. Also, they were cold and figured the effort would warm them up. It did, and we kept at it until about four o'clock when we decided it was time to get back to camp before dark.

Naturally, we thought we would ski down the trail, but it was too steep, lots of turns and falls, and we finally took the skis off again and walked out.

A large campfire was put together and we were able to dry out and prepare our favorite dinner, macaroni and cheese. It was at this point we discovered we had brought only enough food for one night, not two. What a tragedy! We all wanted to go back up to the upper lake, but would have to drive home immediately after skiing, soaking wet, tired and very hungry.

Jack Kirk, meanwhile, had been exploring and discovered a partial sack of potatoes and some mouldy onions in the cook shack. He had also found a partially empty can of Crisco and an old rusty pan. It was obvious that they would not survive the winter as the mice were doing their best to eat them all before spring. Our spirits soared! Tomorrow night we would have fried potatoes and onions!

The entire crew was completely exhausted from the day's efforts so our evening's conversation, while quite animated in discussing our first day's skiing accomplishments didn't last long. We were asleep as soon as we climbed into our sleeping bags.

It was very difficult getting out of our bags in the morning. We were all stiff from unused muscles and several of us had painful leg cramps during the night. Nevertheless, once we were up, we were anxious to get back on the ski slope again. Our efforts of yesterday had greatly facilitated our return, as there was now a well-worn trail, albeit steep, clear to the lake. We arrived at the lake about eleven o'clock and because of yesterday's experience were much drier.

Skiing continued as before, but it became obvious, almost immediately, that we were becoming more adept. A tour of the lake followed, making a track around the lake and up the trail on Baldy Ridge for a couple of hundred yards followed by an exhilarating run back to the lake, periodically broken up by falls. A shorter trail was broken directly across the lake, and we found that most of us were able to herring-bone up our previous practice hill to the start of our trail back to Camp Cleland. What an improvement. We were in great spirits as we bragged about our individual accomplishments and talked about future trips into the Olympics.

Dinner that night was a fitting end to our first skiing experience. When the spoiled parts of the onions and potatoes had been trimmed off there was still more than enough for all of us, and we finished the meal completely satiated. Except for dinner, all conversation centered on today's skiing and future skiing. Once again we were ready for bed, and apparently we had overcome our leg cramps as I heard no shrieks of agony.

In the morning we packed up, cleaned up any sign of our having used Camp Cleland's facilities, and headed home with new thoughts of winter outings.

This was the start of a lifelong skiing friendship for Pete and me. Instead of those monstrous seven foot Northland skis we used at

Lake Lena, Pete now uses 190 cm (6 foot 3 inch) Volkls and I use 195 cm (6 foot 5 inch) Rossignols. We both belong to the "Ancient Skiers" club, founded by skiers who in the thirties traveled to Mt. Rainier every weekend and tore up the ski slopes in Paradise Valley. The club's motto is "pre war-pre tow," and although this is no longer a membership eligibility requirement, the age of 65 and a present or previous residency and skiing experience in the Pacific Northwest is basically it. We enjoy a full week at Sun Valley every January with reduced rates, and no longer have to climb the hill. High speed quads do the job.

CHAPTER 16
VALLEY OF LOST MEN

A winter ascent of The Brothers seemed to be a good idea, as it had never been accomplished, so over Christmas break 1939 Swede Johnson, Don Dooley and I decided that we should make a winter ascent of the South Peak of The Brothers. A weather check predicted that we should have overcast skies for the eastern Olympics, but no precipitation, so conditions seemed to be favorable. We already knew the route, but winter camping away from a Forest Service shelter was new to us, and for the first time we decided to use a tent.

Small tents were available through the Sears-Roebuck catalog, but were designed for summer camping, had no floor or front flap, and were outrageously expensive for high school and college students. Pup tents were no better, and we had almost decided to just go and build a lean-to out of boughs when I recalled my long ago climb of Mt. Ellinor. The Criders and our family had made the climb, and I remembered that the Criders had taken a small three-man tent with them on that occasion.

Nothing ventured, nothing gained. I called up George Crider and after I explained our dilemma, he was more than willing to loan us the tent. His only requirement was that if it became wet, we should dry it out as soon as possible. It was made of silk, and he prized it highly for use on his fishing expeditions. The tent and my kerosene-burning primus stove fixed us right up for winter camping, so we loaded up our packs and skis on my spiffy 1930 Model-A Tudor Ford, complete with a ski rack on the running board, and we were ready.

We left town in mid-morning, stopped at Hoodsport for a hamburger lunch, then continued on to the Lake Lena trailhead on the Hamma Hamma River, arriving there an hour or two later.

The ground was clear of snow, so carrying our skis we started up the trail to the lake. It was just about at the lake level that we came upon occasional patches of snow, and after leaving the lake and traveling up the Valley of Lost Men trail for about a mile, the snow cover began to fill the trail. It was not enough, however, to ski efficiently, and we kept on up the trail for another mile before continuing on skis. We finally arrived at the end of the trail and found about six inches of snow on the ground. It was getting dark by this time, so we made camp. This consisted of cutting a substantial supply of fir boughs and arranging them over the snow on a level area, then pitching the tent over the boughs. Don had thoughtfully brought a candle lantern and this we suspended from the tent ridge. After lighting the primus stove, we brought it inside, set it on a flat rock from the creek, and we were ready for dinner. (The operation of a mountain stove in the tent is not considered good practice today because of the danger from tent fire and the possible asphyxiation from carbon monoxide fumes.)

On the trail.

A little after midnight, Swede, the worrier, awoke and discovered that is was snowing and that the tent was sagging from the snow load. Don and I took care of this by kicking the tent walls, precipitating minor avalanches and promptly went back to sleep. By morning we had done this twice more and discovered we now had an additional six to eight inches of new snow on the ground. Over breakfast of hot oatmeal, we discussed our dilemma. It was obvious we must give up the climb of The Brothers because of the potential avalanche danger. This was a great disappointment. We all hated to go home a day early, as we were well provisioned and enjoying the new experience of winter camping.

The snow had stopped falling by this time, so we put on our skis and started up the route to the South Brother just to see what the conditions were. With skis the going was pretty easy, but when we came to the gully normally used to climb to the summit ridge, we knew we had make the right decision to abandon the climb, so returned to the camp site. Not to be skunked, Swede suggested we ski on up the Valley of Lost Men beyond camp and explore a little. We started, but of course there was no trail, and we wandered back and forth looking for routes clear of logs. This wasn't easy, but with a total accumulation of over a foot of snow, we were able to make a fair amount of progress over minor obstructions and thickets of young hemlocks. Things finally got too difficult for the skis, and we returned to our camp in early afternoon.

The route we had chosen through low underbrush, plus the exertion, left us in a rather damp condition, so the most important item on our agenda at that point was to get dried out. Starting a fire turned out to be rather simple, in as much as we had an ample supply of kerosene fuel along. The rest of the day was spent standing in front of our fire, occasionally snatching our drying socks away from the twigs on which we had suspended them near the fire. The smell of burning wool is an odor a person never forgets!

The snow storm was behind us, and although the temperature dropped to a chilly 20 degrees, we had a comfortable night in our blanket-reinforced summer sleeping bags. In the morning we packed up after breakfast and headed down the trail on skis. In places the trail was quite steep, the snow fairly deep, and as we were unaccustomed to skiing with packs, it was tough going. After many falls we arrived at Lake Lena where travel improved greatly on the wide, fairly level trail. At the top of the logged-off hill down to the trailhead, we took the skis off and walked to the car, thankful that we had survived our retreat unscathed.

There were about five inches of new snow on the road, but the old Model-A fired right up, and we were on our way to civilization. Our feeling of relaxation was short lived, though, as at the first uphill grade we stalled out. There was nothing for it, but to put on chains and try again. About eight miles later, after much pushing and some riding, we made it out to the highway. After all that effort to extricate my Ford, we agreed we had earned something, stopped at Hoodsport on our way back to Bremerton and treated ourselves to apple pie ala mode and milkshakes. The only chore left was to dry George Crider's tent.

I am a loyal reader of Robert L. Wood's fascinating accounts of the O'Neil expedition in 1890 and Press expedition the preceding year. I have also enjoyed his accurate description of ways and byways in his *Olympic Mountains Trail Guide*. It was in this guide that he related the origin of *"The Valley of Silent Men"* named for the trail we had just travelled. Apparently this came about because a climbing party from Olympic College had become winded from their exertions on the trail, with no breath left for conversation. When they finally got their breathing in control, they named the trail after their experience.

This certainly occurred, but I believe the real name of the trail relates to *"The Valley of Lost Men,"* named earlier by the Boy Scouts at Camp Cleland on Lake Lena when the camp director, prior to World War II, was Tom Martin (no relation to George). One of the scouts, Jerry Sampels of Shelton, and another scout became lost in this valley, and it was promptly named *"The Valley of Lost Men"* by the scouts at camp - and thereafter, a legend. I got this information directly from the ultimate authority, Jim Phillips, former scout executive of the *Tumwater Council, BSA,* and the recognized unofficial historian of the council. Both names are appropriate, both are true, and a person may choose whichever name he prefers. I personally like *"The Valley of Lost Men,"* as it was not only named first, but also has an aura of mystery that has a certain appeal.

South Peak after a heavy snowfall.

CHAPTER 17
MT. STONE

After a long, hard winter chasing down the elusive "Mt.Lincoln Ski Bowl" plus other week-ends skiing at Mt. Rainier, several of us felt we should do a little mountain climbing as a change of pace. After all, there's nothing like summer in the Olympics.

My friend Chet Ullin, a counselor at Camp Cleland, had recommended Mt.Stone as a good climb. There were four of us; Chuck Thompson, Bill Eldridge, Harry Winsor and me in the party. As all of us were working or going to school it was decided to utilize the long holiday week-end of Memorial Day, May 29,30 and 31, 1937. We wanted to make the most of this precious time so we cheated a bit and took off from Bremerton right after work on Friday, May 28th, drove to the trail head on the Hamma Hamma and stayed in the as yet unoccupied Camp Cleland that night.

Our packs weren't particularly heavy, but Chuck and I had added one additional item we had never taken with us before - short "summer" skis, only three feet long, with bear trap toe irons and leather heal straps tightened with bilstein heal latches. We had also added heavy elastic rubber straps to hold our heals tight against the skis if desired. The skis, when secured under the cover flap of our Trapper Nelson packs, presented no transportation problems.

Saturday morning saw us up before the sun and we were on our way up the trail to Upper Lake Lena by about 7:30. It promised to be a beautiful day, with clear skies and occasional small cumulous clouds here and there. Our trip was uneventful until about a mile below Upper Lake Lena when we reached the first snow drifts. They presented no difficulties and by the time we reached the upper lake, about nine o'clock, the residual winter snow was everywhere. The lake was open, however, and the sunny day was expected to soften up the snow surface.

We continued around the lake with Mt. Baldy (now named Mt.

Lena) on our right, trying out our summer skis and finding them rather difficult to control on the hard, frozen surface of the snow. The way to Mt. Stone climbed steadily after leaving the lake. Our amateurish efforts on the skis were a hindrance and eventually off came the skis and resumption of the climb in softening snow from the increasing intensity of the sun as the day progressed. The trail, of course, was hidden beneath the snow cover but the route was obvious and we proceeded on foot to the top of what we called Baldy Ridge in those days. Mt. Bretherton, on our left, was quite impressive, and we discussed climbing it after we had returned from Mt. Stone if we had time.

Above Upper Lake Lena.

From here our route dropped down the west side of the ridge and headed in a southerly direction with Mt. Stone rising prominently on the horizon and getting closer by the minute. We were now in a narrow valley between Mt. Stone and Baldy Ridge, and our way became more difficult as we progressed, with occasional low cliffs and steep slopes to be overcome. Because of the winter snow, however, we were able to select routes that avoided most of these hazards, and thankfully all underbrush thickets were covered with snow.

We reached Deerheart Lake about noon, and although it was frozen a creek flowing into its east side was open and provided water. It was decided to camp here as Chuck wanted to drop down to Scout Lake, situated about 800 feet directly below us, on our skis. Harry and Bill, as they had no skis, decided to stay at the lake. We, in the skiing party, without packs, started down the slope.

The grade initially was gentle, and with all of the snow cover we were skiing well, although stability was much less than we had been accustomed to on longer "winter" skis. There were frequent falls because of our inability to turn on the now heavy corn snow, and by the time we had dropped about 400 feet it was getting increasingly steep with occasional vertical drops of forty or fifty feet. At this point I suggested we give up on Scout Lake, and Chuck said "I'm glad you said something. I was in the process of trying to figure out what to say that wouldn't make me seem chicken." Chuck smiled, reached down to take off his skis, and I followed suit.

The return to camp was a long, dry haul. The snow had now softened up to a point where we sank in six or seven inches every step and had to rotate turns at trail breaking about every hundred steps.

Finally we got back to the others and our packs, to find them confortably relaxed and sun bathing on their sleeping bags with a generous five or six inch bed of fir boughs underneath. We were tired after the long haul back to camp, but after quenching our huge thirst got to work making our own beds.

Making camp was quite simple. The weather forecast for the whole weekend was for clear skies so we were not concerned with rain, and stamped out flat places in the snow, covered them with generous quantities of boughs, and that was camp. Near the lake Harry had dug down to the top of a rock outcropping, and we had our fire pit. The dry weather was on our side as far as fire was concerned, so squaw brush and dead branches from spruce and fir trees served admirably for fuel. Chuck, always the connoisseur of fine foods, had prepared a gourmet dinner—macaroni and cheese with coffee and dried prunes.

The rest of the evening was spent relaxing on our sleeping bags or searching Mt. Stone for possible climbing routes the next day, then discussing or arguing our various assault plans. With sundown came a definite drop in the temperature and we were all glad to climb into sleeping bags to stay warm. Bill and I suffered leg cramps during the night, but not enough to keep us awake much.

Because of the softening of the snow we had decided to get a very early start to provide good travel conditions for most of the day. Without packs or skis we were off up the small valley at daybreak, traveling south for about a mile. At this point the little valley terminated in a saddle, and our route dropped down very abruptly two or three hundred feet into a fairly large bowl with a couple of small lakes, partially cleared of ice. At that time they were unnamed, but now are called Stone Ponds. The saddle we had passed through is now called Stone Pond Pass.

From here it was all uphill. We could see St. Peter's Gate, a prominent col about 3/8 mile ahead that we were to pass through. Our route was still southerly, and St. Peter's Gate was between the east flank of Mt. Stone's South Peak and another point to the east, although less prominent than Mt. Stone. It was still early morning when we started the climb over as yet crusted snow, offering good footing and we made excellent progress over the large snowfield that filled the entire valley, from Stone Ponds to the Gate.

At the pass we rested for awhile, had candy bars, ate snow, and enjoyed the view. To the north we could see Baldy (Mt. Lena) in the distance, completely covered with snow and to the northeast the imposing Mt. Bretherton. Chuck said we must surely climb this on our way back to the car.

It was at this exact spot, many years later, that my climbing buddy from Alaska, Rod Wilson, his brother George and I were resting when a trio of mountain goats reached us. They had dogged (goated) our footsteps all the way from Stone Ponds, where we had camped. They were not the least afraid, coming within ten feet of us without hesitation. We had set our Kelty packs upright in the snow, and were sitting on an adjacent rock ledge eating a snack and watching them approach. They went immediately to our packs and licked the packstraps, a goat per pack, for about five minutes, obviously for the salty perspiration on the straps. We surmised that they did this to every hiker who passed through St. Peter's Gate. One of them decided that he needed more salt than licking provided, and tried to eat the strap. Rod jumped down and made for the goat, chasing it away. Another of the goats, at this point, charged Rod, but chickened out at the last moment. The young goat who had tried to improve his salt intake was obviously the second goat's adult kid, and she was demonstrating her instinctive child protection. We decided it was time to go, so put on our packs and started down without the goats toward the Lake of The Angels, our goal for that night.

Chet Ullin had described the route he used to climb Mt. Stone, a first ascent, as follows: "Pass through St. Peter's Gate, dropping down the south side for two or three hundred feet, then turn right at the base of Mt. Stone's south cliffs and traverse under them, gradually climbing until the cliffs are gone - about a quarter of a mile - then turn right, in a northerly direction toward the summit. A brief scramble will see you on top." We followed exactly as he suggested, in snow the whole distance and the obvious route. The final scramble was over rock, not snow, and the summit was ours, at an elevation of 6612 feet.

By the time we had reached the peak the sun was out in full force. Fortunately a trickle of snow melt was running down the face of an exposed rock and we all quenched our thirst, albeit with great difficulty. More candy bars were devoured, and we gloated in our successful climb. The view to the north was enhanced from this vantage point. Everything we had seen from St. Peter's Gate was there, but also the Middle Peak could be seen, only 12 feet lower. To the south was Mt. Skokomish, with Mt. Gladys and Sawtooth Ridge in the distance, and Mt's. Jefferson, Pershing, Washington and Ellinor to the southeast. The whole Hamma Hamma Valley was before us to the east, with Hood Canal and Puget Sound beyond. Mt. Rainier as usual was very dominant.

We had discussed climbing the Middle Peak as well, but now vetoed this. Harry, the smart one, could forsee a troublesome trip back to camp if the sun softened up the snow the way it had the previous day. With this thought in mind we left the summit and retraced our steps. The short climb back up to the Gate was already softening up to the point that we were taking turns trail breaking and we knew our troubles were just beginning. Bill Eldridge made the comment, "Paul, we should have remembered our Lake LaCrosse hike two years ago, and avoided all this." He was right. We should have.

South Peak.

North Peak from South Peak (Mt. Stone).

A rest was taken at the top of the col, and then we started down, everyone on his own toward Stone Ponds. I left the Gate last, and soon the grade increased to the point that I thought sitting down and sliding in this position would be superior to glissading, as the snow was really too soft for that. Sure enough, it was better. I zipped right on by the others, bringing a huge amount of heavy, wet show with me. When I got far enough down the snowfield to slow down, the snow that followed closed in around me, burying me to my armpits, and we, the snow and I, came to a halt.

I found that I was encased in snow, as hard as concrete, burying me above my waist, and pressing in with considerable force. I immediately called out to the others not to do as I had, and fortunately they escaped the concrete encasement. My hands and arms were still free, and with the help of the others I was able to extricate myself. I shudder to think what would have happened if my arms had also been encased, or if I had been alone - a valuable lesson in snow conditions that my friends and I never forgot.

We were almost down to Stone Ponds, so we stopped for a much needed drink of water, then moved on to the trudge up to Stone Pond Pass. The sun, about mid-afternoon on a south-facing slope, certainly didn't do us a good turn. It was a long, exhausting drag back to camp.

The next morning came with more sunshine, and we felt we should be at Upper Lena Lake not later than noon to avoid more soft snow, but as it was only about two miles to the lake from camp we knew that we had ample time. We had also vetoed climbing Mt. Bretherton, so after a leisurely oatmeal and prune breakfast we climbed back up to the top of Baldy ridge. Chuck thought we might ski down the more or less gentle slopes from here to Upper Lena Lake.

No sooner said than done, on went the skis. Believe me, that idea was a disaster. With packs and those summer skis it was impossible to travel more than a hundred feet or so before falling, and turning was out of the question. Chuck again was the first to remove his skis, and I was right behind him. Fortunately the snow hadn't softened too much, and we were at the lake before noon.

It seemed a shame to waste the rest of the day, so we agreed to practice our ski technique, without packs, to facilitate easier trips in the future. We returned to the gentle slopes just above the lake. It had been extremely warm all week-end, and we - all except Harry, the smart one - took off shirts and long pants, and Chuck and I proceeded to ski in shorts and boots and get a little tan. That's what we got, and a lot of sunburn. Two hours of ski practice and I discovered I was a sunburn basket case, as did the others (except Harry). We dressed again, and with packs the source of extreme agony made our way slowly back to the trailhead and our car.

We were all of us, except Harry, too badly burned to work for the next two days. My back and shoulders were a mass of runny yellow blisters, and my face was practically one big scab.

This was a marvelous climb, discounting everything that happened thereafter, and we all agreed it had been extremely instructional; first, the danger of heavy snow avalanches, and second, alpine sunburn. I have remembered and avoided such dangers ever since.

Baldy Ridge above Upper Lake Lena (Memorial Day 1937).

CHAPTER 18
THE BROTHERS

Early in the summer of 1936, while admiring George Martin's latest photographic efforts of the Hurricane Ridge near Port Angeles, we began a discussion about The Brothers, a prominent peak on the western Olympic skyline. George stated that he had often wanted to make the climb, and we should do it. The best time seemed to be over Labor Day weekend, as most of our group had jobs and the three-day holiday seemed like a good target date.

The party ultimately assembled consisted of George, myself, Chuck Thompson, Chuck's brother Jack, Bob Scott, and Harry Winsor. I was the only member who had climbed the mountain before so I was designated guide, and George our leader. We planned to camp on the summit of the South Peak, so we all packed lightly as we had a steep narrow gully to ascend with an elevation change of over 3,500 feet and another 300 feet more along the ridge above the gully.

For this reason we left Bremerton at an early hour and proceeded by car to the trailhead below Lower Lena Lake. The trail up to the lake was uneventful. At the north end of the lake, after passing Camp Cleland on the west shore, the trail to the base of The Brothers branched off to the east, and we followed up the East Fork of Lena Creek for about three miles where it terminated and the climb began. As a sidelight, I am told that some hikers got lost overnight up this trail many years ago, and the area then became known to the scouts at Camp Cleland as "The Valley of Lost Men"—a legend that must have been retold year after year at Camp Cleland campfires.

We knew that there would be no water beyond this point, so we filled up the canteens and water bottles we had brought with us, and then were ready for the climb. As I mentioned earlier, it was steep, and places where we could stop and rest without packs on our backs were difficult to find. Several hours later we topped out and took a real rest.

Looking west at sunset from bivouac.

The weather was beautiful, a photographer's dream, so the first thing George did was pull out his giant speed-graflex press camera (with tripod) from his pack and start taking his famous pictures. The sun was still up in the southwest, so he concentrated on shots to the east, covering most of Puget Sound.

We had another few hundred feet to climb to a suitable camp site near the summit, so we reluctantly continued the climb up the ridge to the north. When we were near our camp site, I noted a snow patch in a gully down the west side of the ridge, perhaps 100 yards away. As soon as we reached camp, I emptied my *Trapper Nelson* and returned for a load of snow. I caught all kinds of comments about how sanitary was my pack, and what had I previously carried in it? They didn't appear to be too happy when I informed them that I had transported my neighbor's puppies in it the previous week!

George continued his photography after dinner, working on the setting sun behind Mt. Stone on the horizon. Our weather was unbelievable; cloudless, warm even at 6,800 feet elevation, and the afterglow seemed to linger forever. As it began to darken in the east we could see the first stars appear, and a dark shadow rapidly approached us - the edge of night. I will never forget that evening as long as I live.

Next morning before daybreak George was up again, getting set up for sunrise, and it turned out as spectacular as the sunset the nightbefore. All of Puget Sound to the east was entirely covered with a bank of clouds, the top of the layer about a thousand feet below us. The eastern skyline was broken with the volcanic cones of Mt. Baker, Glacier Peak, Mt. Rainier and Mt. St. Helens - fully as awesome as last night's marvelous display.

The true south summit was a quarter of a mile and about 300 feet higher than our campsite, so after a leisurely breakfast and another trip for snow we left to put our names in the summit cairn, then to continue on north along the ridge separating us from the north Brother. Our route dropped a little to the east of the ridge, mainly on wide heather-covered ledges, with a final rock scramble to the top of the south Brother. This was practically a stroll, and we celebrated the occasion with George taking more pictures.

Summit of the South Peak from bivouac.

After leaving the south peak, we dropped down to the east side of the saddle between the two summits and again traversed north on numerous comfortable ledges until we were under the north peak. A scramble completed the climb, and we had our lunch.

The cloud cover over Puget Sound had burned off by this time, and we enjoyed a perfect view of Seattle and ships on the sound. The entire eastern skyline was dominated by the major volcanic peaks, with the sections between filled in with the beautiful Cascade Range, clear and sharp even from a distance of 60 or 70 miles. To the west could be seen Mt. Olympus, Mt. Anderson and scores of other peaks. A truly breathtaking site.

Our return to camp was leisurely, and in the early evening we arrived at camp. I made another trip for snow and the others argued about who would prepare dinner. I was exempt. I was the snowman. After dinner - macaroni and cheese, of course - we all located comfortable seats and spent the evening enjoying again the previous evening's observations. In the morning weather conditions duplicated those of the day before, and after sunup and breakfast we packed up and started the descent to "The Valley of Lost Men" and ultimately home.

George's pictures were a complete success, as was the entire climb - no problems, all goals met and wonderful weather. They should all go so well!

(Author's Note: It was recently pointed out to me that the traverse between the two peaks is graded in "The Climbers' Guide to the Olympic Mountains" as a class 4. My experience on this was made almost 60 years ago and memories fade, but I still can't recall anything more difficult than class 3. It is still a scramble to the best of my memory.)

Bivouacked near the summit.

SECTION V

Mt. Olympus Massif
(Quadrant 4 Map)

QUADRANT 4 MAP

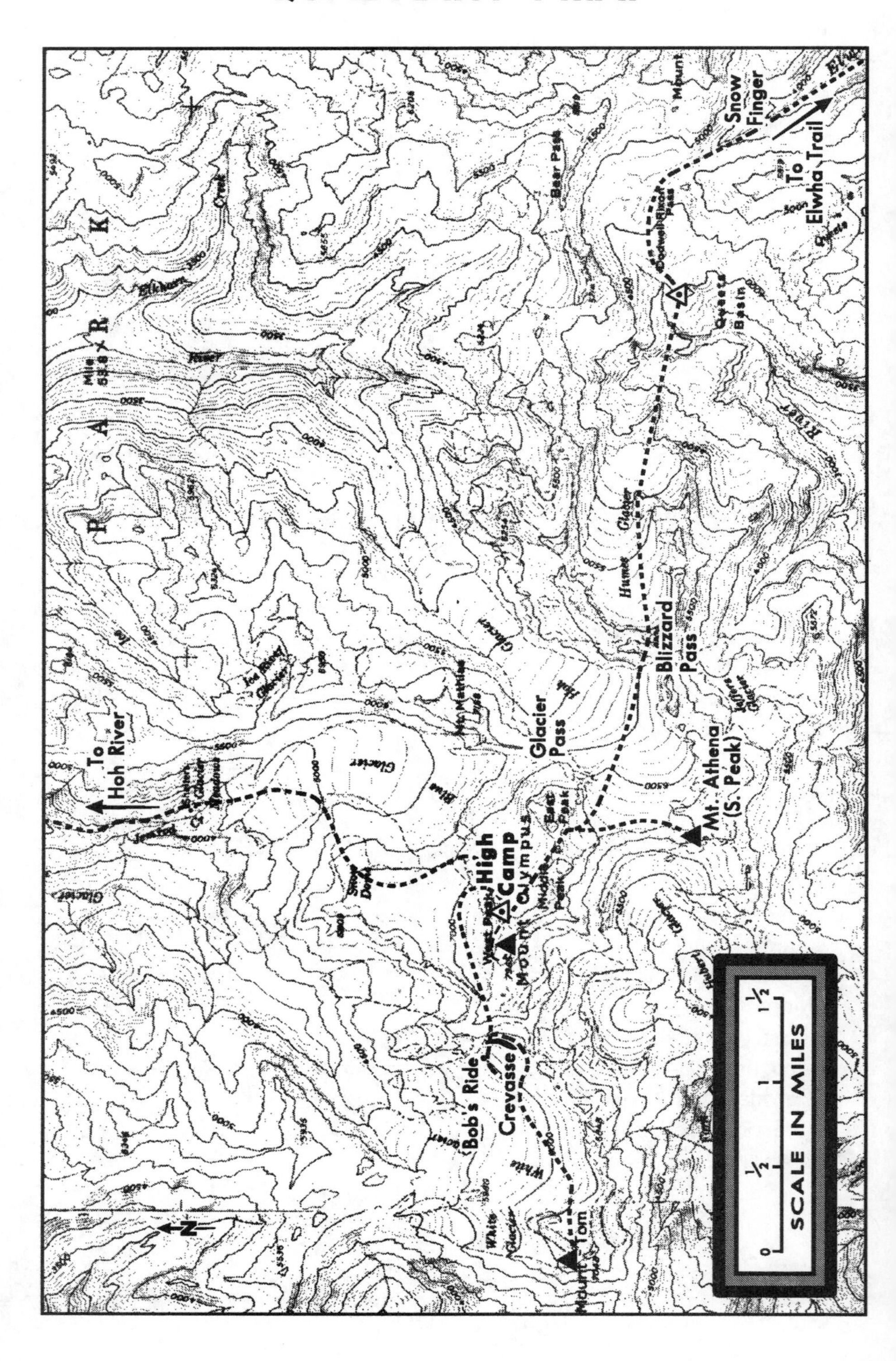

CHAPTER 19
OLYMPUS TRAVERSE

The ascent of Mt. Olympus, the high point in the entire Olympic Mountain Range, is probably the goal of every climber who has succumbed to the mountain's siren call. George Martin had been promoting a Mt. Olympus climb for a couple of years, and immediately after school was out in 1937 and his teaching duties for the year were behind him he contacted a number of members of our local climbing group. He succeeded in pulling together a team of five - George plus Jim Swanson, a friend of George's in the Methodist Church, Carl Rusher, Harry Winsor, and me.

We all met at George's house and he presented his plan, the climb to be in July. It was to be for a week's duration, starting out from Solduc Hot Springs, climbing the mountain - all three peaks - then coming out down the Hoh Valley. This sounded great, but at that point I made the off-hand suggestion that we might change our escape route, make a traverse of the mountain and come out via the Queets, Elwha and Dosewallips Rivers. This sounded even better after I made a verbal outline of the proposed trip. We would hike in from Solduc Hot Springs, passing Hoh Lake and Glacier Meadows enroute to the Blue Glacier. From here we would cross that glacier and climb the Snow Dome to the upper glacier and the West Summit. We would camp all night near the summit, then climb the Middle and East peaks and descend the Hoh Glacier to Blizzard Pass and the Humes Glacier to the Queets Basin. Our route from there would take us up the Basin to the historic Dodwell-Rixon Pass and Elwha Snow Finger, down the Elwha to Hayes river camp, over Hayden Pass to the Dosewallips River and out to the trailhead. This idea was particularly appealing because we would not have to drive a car around to the west side of the Olympic Peninsula for return transportation to Bremerton.

The suggestion for the alternative route was prompted by

information I had gleaned in Joseph T. Hazard's book, *Snow Sentinals of the Pacific Northwest* which I had practically memorized I had read it so much. Hazard had described the route we were taking to the summits of Mt. Olympus, but had also detailed the route from Queets Basin to the summit. Although this second description was the reverse of our proposed route, all the details were the same.

Food lists were prepared, climbing equipment gathered and we awaited the great day. I had purchased a small kerosene-fueled primus stove earlier in the summer and we would use this for our high camp on Mt Olympus, no wood being available for fuel. Our departure was on a bright, sunshiny day in two cars. George drove to the Dosewallips trail head, where he left his for our return. Carl Rusher and the rest of us followed, and after picking up George all five of us crowded into Carl's father's big old Oldsmobile Sedan and it was very tight. A couple of the packs were inside, but the rest were tied on to the front fenders.

The hot springs was thankfully reached, and after eating our brown bag lunches from home we were off up the trail. Our first night's camp was scheduled to be Deer Lake, a five mile hike. We arrived there in the middle of the afternoon, tired enough from our first day's efforts to want to make camp. Jim Swanson and I, the only fishermen in the group, did some casting from the lake shore, and Jim finally caught about a 10 inch trout. I was skunked. It went well with our rice dinner that night, however.

About the only disaster of the trip occurred on this segment. The kerosene fuel for my primus stove was carried in a pint bottle with a screw-top. This had come loose, and about half of my pack's contents was soaked with kerosene. At least a third of the lost fuel was now in my spare clothes, tooth brush, and other necessary items. Fortunately the food I carried was above the kerosene line, and although slightly tainted by fumes was still palatable. My sleeping bag also survived. Needless to say I smelled like a repair garage for the rest of the trip.

After breakfast we took off up the trail, still with good weather, our goal for the day only about five miles away at Hoh Lake. Above Deer Lake the trail climbed steadily through timber for about a thousand feet, then broke out into alpine meadows and small tarn lakes that instantly

East Peak from Hoh Glacier - Glacier Pass - Mt. Mathius.

got George's and Harry's attention. They were both dedicated photographers and this was something they didn't want to miss. George as expected pulled his 4x5 Graflex camera out of his pack, also film slides that went with it, and proceeded to put in black and white what we were seeing in a gorgeous chromatic display of July alpine flowers. His equipment must have weighed close to five pounds but he insisted on carrying it without complaint. Harry's camera was much lighter and of later vintage, but his quality of photography couldn't exceed George's .

When the photographers were repacked we continued our climb. The trail swung to the right, slowly climbing the meadows in a long uphill traverse. After about a mile we reached the top of the ridge and George and Harry did their thing again. We were on top of the divide between the Solduc and Hoh rivers - the Bogachiel Trail. This scenic route traverses the ridge top from west to east, alternating between views of the Seven Lakes Basin on the north and Mt. Olympus on the south side of the Hoh Valley. Bogachiel Ridge and its extension, the High Divide, provide access to some of the most beautiful parts of the Olympic Mountains.

A leisurely pace adapted to the great scenery was taken along the ridge for about three miles when we came to the junction with the Hoh Lake trail. We turned off here, to the south, and the trail dropped swiftly into the Hoh Valley. About a mile farther and we arrived at Hoh Lake, our destination for the second day. A beautiful site was found for our camp, and while Carl was gathering wood for dinner George and Harry were getting out their cameras for the new angle shots of Mt. Olympus. Jim and I got out our fishing tackle, and although we tried all the lures we had nothing worked.

A group of people who were camped around the lake from us watched us for awhile, and one of the young men walked over, obviously to discuss fishing. He explained that his party had been at the lake for several days and had caught a number of large trout. Their method was vastly different from ours, however. They had used heavy sinkers and worms for bait. They had cast as far out in the lake as they could and had let the bait settle to the bottom. Their line was then secured to shore and they returned to their camp, occasionally checking to see if they had caught anything. He stated that "The fish are all at the bottom where it is cool. There are no fish at the surface" and he was right. We weren't inclined to fish his method so we returned to our camp to enjoy the view. George and Harry got a lot of sunset shots of Olympus that night, and more in the morning at sunrise.

When photography and breakfast were behind us we continued our journey on down the switchbacking trail to the Hoh River trail about five miles away. At this point we were at a lower elevation than Soleduck Hot Springs where we had started! Our route turned left (east) up the Hoh trail through heavy old growth timber, steadily climbing, and in about three or four miles came to a bridge that crossed the Hoh River over a gorge that must be a hundred feet deep. It was quite an impressive sight. Still climbing, we passed the Elk Lake shelter, then broke out of timber and into Glacier Meadows at about 4500 feet. A shelter was located here, and it became our home for the night.

The view of Mt. Olympus, of course, was spectacular. The good weather was holding, and we could see the Blue Glacier immediately before us, gaining in elevation to the south, then turning west quite

Blue Glacier Ice Fall - Mt. Olympus in clouds beyond.

On Olympus summit ridge.

abruptly, and rising in a gigantic ice fall with huge crevasses almost to the summit snow fields. To the right, north of a rocky cleaver separating the ice fall, is a route finder's dream—a virtually crevasse-free smooth surface to the summit of Mt. Olympus—the Snow Dome! In my mind's eye I could follow our route tomorrow to the summit of the West Peak.

Our weather the next day was phenomenal. When we got up a million stars were out, and we just knew it would be a great day. We got a very early start, five men on one rope, as we hoped to get most of today's climb behind us before the sun softened the snow appreciably. Our route we had chosen yesterday proved to be the right one. The grade of the snow dome varied, from quite steep at the bottom to flattening out at the top where it transitioned into a slightly rising field, sparsely but visibly crevassed. We passed through these to the notch in the ridge that angled down in a northeast direction from the West Summit. Beyond this notch we found ourselves on another smaller field, the upper extreme of the Blue Glacier ice fall, and turning right (west) we shortly reached the east side of the West Peak in a pass in the summit ridge. A steep snow field lead from here up to the spire.

Dumping our packs in the pass, then kicking steps up the snow field, we were soon at the base of the final climb. A series of well-placed and firm hand and foot holds on the northwest side of the spire gave us easy access to the cairn. We had all made it to the highest point in the Olympic Mountains! George said he was going to have to return to his pack and get his camera, but Harry smiled as he took his camera from around his neck and got summit shots of all of us on the spot. After we got this summit posturing out of the way a descent was made back to our packs, and all of us but George began looking for a suitable campsite. There was none immediately visible, but on top of the ridge we had skirted earlier we found not only flat areas suitable for sleeping, but also pools of water in hollows of the rocks, residual melting from earlier snow cover. We were all fixed up for the night.

When George got back we organized camp and I fired up the primus stove. Man, it really worked! No wood gathering, no working with wet wood, just light it! A minor breeze had its effect on the stove, however, and we discovered that we had to shield it with packboards if it was to work properly. This was incidental, and the stove was a real success.

After dinner we put on all the clothes we had (kerosene and all) because of the sudden fall in temperature as the sun dropped into the Pacific Ocean far to the west. It was fascinating and a rare experience, but we cut the viewing short because of the temperature change.

Another bright morning greeted us, but it was cold. It must have been after 7 o'clock when we felt we could face the world. It was much warmer than the night before, though. The little primus performed perfectly again and and our oatmeal breakfast was soon over, we packed up, and after George climbed the peak once more we were off to a long day ahead.

We had in mind climbing all three Olympus summits this day. Although my memory after fifty years is a little hazy, as I recall our route on the summit ridge led to Middle Peak, which we reached after traversing across the relatively flat upper end of the Blue Glacier. The summit was ours after a scramble up the west side.

Descending from the Middle Peak we dropped down off the ridge a short distance to the south onto the Hoh Glacier until we were below the East Peak, where we dropped our packs. After a rather tedious climb up a steep snow field on the southeast side of the East Peak we claimed that summit too. George again carried his heavy camera to this summit, although he was starting to ration his few remaining film slides. He said he just couldn't miss something we hadn't observed before.

Upon returning to our packs we started the descent of the upper Hoh Glacier. There were numerous large crevasses, but well defined and we had no difficulty in avoiding them. After traveling about two miles down the glacier we reached the point on the south margin of the glacier that I assumed was Blizzard Pass, our access to the Humes Glacier. Joe Hazard had stated in his book that there was a steep 700 foot wall to climb to reach the Humes Glacier, and this looked like it. As I wasn't positive though, I decided to reconnoiter first, so I said I would leave my pack and climb up alone to be sure we were right.

When I made this statement I thought for a moment that George would swear, or do something else just as drastic. I have never heard him curse, but I think he was on the verge. He asked, in a slightly elevated voice, "Do you mean, Paul, that you've never been here before?" I replied that of course I hadn't. I then had to explain Joe Hazard's description of his route in his book. He replied, "Well, you've done O.K. so far, Let's not change anything now." Then he smiled, and all was well although I did feel a little guilty about the misunderstanding.

Sure enough, after investigation the spot I had picked was not Blizzard Pass. It led instead to Jeffers Glacier and the Queets River beyond. My view from there did let me see the real Blizzard Pass, though, and after I descended we trudged over to it and started the 700 foot climb. When we reached the pass we could see an obvious route down to the Humes Glacier. There were about two miles of glacier to descend, with only a couple of crevasses showing near the bottom. When we reached the rock wall at the glacier snout it presented some difficult problems, but by rappelling we made it past them. From here on it was a rather steep descent of about a mile on the ridge leading from the snout to the lower Queets basin. This concluded our very strenuous day, and we made camp in good spirits.

We were now back to alpine meadows, clumps of spruce and fir trees, and a burbling river nearby. We were also in Elk Heaven, and droppings were everywhere. The odor was more like a barn yard than an alpine paradise, but everything else about the place seemed like a human alpine heaven. It was absolutely beautiful, with our fabulous weather still with us. later in the evening we saw a heard of fifty or sixty elk grazing a couple of hundred yards on down the Queets river. The best part of the whole transition from glacier to meadow, however, was George's comment, "Paul, you've done a great job getting us here."

It took the sun longer than usual the next morning to reach our camp because of our location in the Queets Basin. It did appear eventually with its warming rays and we were soon up, breakfasted, packed and away. There were about a thousand feet for us to climb from our camp to the top of Dodwell-Rixon Pass, the headwaters of the Elwha River, but after our previous trek earlier in the week this was not a serious problem. We marveled as we progressed at the sudden transition in the terrain from the meadows at our camp to the barren, desolate landscape around us. Both Mt. Barnes to the north of Dodwell-Rixon Pass and Mt. Queets to the south had timber on their lower slopes, and there were meadows showing to the north just below Bear Glacier. otherwise it was a stark, sterile area. We pondered the absence of all vegetation, and even George had no real answer. There apparently wasn't enough top soil for anything to grow.

Harry Winsor on West Peak summit.

Dodwell-Rixon Pass was eventually reached and after a short break we started down the snow finger that led us to the Elwha Basin. It was easy going, a good walkway, although we could see sections where the river's erosion from below and the sun's melting above had joined forces to leave dangerous, gaping holes in the surface. There were undoubtedly also some thin spots that hadn't as yet broken through.

This prompted us to stay on the edges, although there was also some melting back from there also. Nevertheless we had a very uneventful journey, not even encountering any problems in getting off the the snow finger's snout. This calls to mind another trip, this time with my son Peter (not to be confused with Pete, my climbing friend) when we made the Bailey Range Traverse several years ago. We had camped in the meadows in Bear Pass next to Bear Glacier, and from this high perch could look across the desolate upper Queets Basin to the ravine where Dodwell-Rixon Pass was located. Having been here before I anticipated an easy hike out. We dropped down from Bear Pass, traversed the barren basin, and approached the pass.

What a transformation since my first visit! There was no snow finger- just a rushing stream clogged with rocks and hundreds of logs piled up like jack straws as far down the river as we could see. This made extremely difficult traveling. We were at it all day. Finally in late afternoon Peter took off his pack and climbed the gravel cliff to the north to reach the timbered slopes looking for an easier route. He returned with the good news that he had found a game trail that appeared to go down the river, basically paralleling it. This certainly beat what we doing in the riverbed, so we moved to the trees and with Peter leading we dropped down about a quarter of a mile until we came to the beginning of a real trail. There was a campsite at this location and we immediately stopped and made camp. I was completely exhausted although Peter was obviously not nearly as tired as I.

But to get back to our present uneventful jaunt down the snow finger; we stepped off of the snow and found ourselves in another sub-alpine meadow, so thick with wild flowers of all colors that there were more colored blossoms than green grass showing. To compound the glorious view were the peaks of Mts. Queets, Barnes, Meany, Seattle,

Noyes and Christie providing a very impressive wall to the south, Enclosing the Elwha Basin and beckoning us to their summits. This was the ideal time to stop, rest, and enjoy, so we did all of these, and had lunch too.

Our trip schedule required us to be at Hayes River camp this evening. Hayes River was still 12 miles away and it was noon, so glorious vistas or not we must be on our way. We now had a genuine, first class trail to follow and we really burned up the miles. Shortly after leaving our lunch site the meadow ended and we were once more in a large virgin forest. This shut out the sun almost entirely, and for the first time in three days we did not need to worry about sun paint and sunburn.

It was at least five in the evening when we arrived at Hayes River camp. We now noticed that while we had been in the shadows of the forest on the trail it was becoming overcast. Our good weather for the preceding five days had been a godsend to our expedition, but had also been unusual. No one griped about the change in the weather, just thankful that we had a nice dry forest service shelter for the night.

Jim and I got out our fishing tackle to try the Elwha River, and sure enough the trout were as plentyful as I had found it six years before. They also still liked my little black beetles. We gathered all the dry wood we could find for the evening, and had a real campfire that night. This camp was the end of our trip as far as our Olympus venture was concerned. From here on it would be just a lot of walking.

It started raining during the night, and continued on through breakfast. There was still plenty of kerosene left so we cooked on the primus stove - oatmeal, of course - and after breakfast, in raincoats, started up the trail towards Hayden Pass. This was a long, uphill climb and we were mostly quiet. About ten the rain stopped and we thankfully put the sweat-drenched rain gear back in our packs. Soon thereafter the sub alpine terrain began to change, and the meadows and clumps of spruce trees took over. The sun began to appear, too, through our cloud cover, and all was well again.

Shortly after noon we reached Hayden Pass and enjoyed one of the great sights in the Olympics, the huge meadow expanse of Dose Meadows and the thousand acre meadows. In the distance could be seen Mt. Constance, The Brothers, Mt. Stone and many others, old friends in this sea of peaks.

We had lunch in the pass, then started on down the Dosewallips River trail, passing through meadows and disturbing a group of three deer, as well as at least half a dozen marmots whose shrill whistles sounded like a section of flutes all tuning up to a different key. Farther down, on the slopes near the Lost Pass trail, we saw a bear ambling up the slope away from us.

Camp for the night was at Camp Marion and we used up the last of the kerosene for dinner. We had a delicacy for that last evening - macaroni and cheese! In the morning we decided not to cook oatmeal (it was getting pretty old), but instead to have a cold breakfast—some cheese, dried prunes and apricots, rye crisp biscuits and the remaining jam. This included the last of our lunches, so if we didn't want to stop and make a fire to cook oatmeal our next meal would be in civilization.

George's car, which we had left at the Dosewallips trailhead earlier on our way to Solduc Hot Springs, was fourteen miles away but it was all downhill, we were now in exceptional physical condition, and our packs were lighter. We made it in early afternoon - the culmination of George's dream two years before.

Now came the anti-climax. He had to drive all of us and packs to the Brinnon Ferry, then drive with Carl to Solduc hot springs to retrieve Carl's car, then all the way to Bremerton. The rest of us phoned Bremerton from Brinnon, and Jim Swanson's wife met us at Seabeck for our ride home. So ended a happy trip. *NOTE: Our glacier travel, according to current practice, was extremely hazardous, and there wasn't an ice axe or pair of crampons among us. Further, five on a rope is considered extremely poor practice. All I can say is that what we did then was the norm for the period. Professionally guided climbs, of course, such as summit climbs on Mt. Rainier had stricter requirments. I know we wouldn't try this same trip today without proper equipment and techniques. This was my first use of a mountain stove on this trip and I wouldn't be without one now. I strongly recommend against stoves using kerosene for fuel, however, for obvious reasons. Gasoline fuel, if spilled, will evaporate with no lingering odor or taste.*

CHAPTER 20
MTS. OLYMPUS, TOM AND ATHENA

Pete Pedersen, my earliest friend and fellow skier, hiker and climber herewith tells of one of his most memorable summers in the Olympic Mountains. Just reading of his experiences is almost as exciting as having been there with him. Here are his stories:

By R.A.Pedersen

The summer of 1938 turned out to be one of the most rewarding summer climbing seasons in my life, leaving many happy memories for my old age. As a 20-year-old college student just returned from a month-long midshipmen's cruise I was anxious to get started climbing. To my good fortune a small group of friends consisting of George Martin, Bob Scott, Paul Crews and Harry Winsor invited me to join them on a warm-up climb of Mt. St. Helens. This was in early July and was followed by a climb of Mt. Constance with a large group of Bremerton Ski Cruisers. In early August a small group of us made a 7-day traverse through the Eastern Olympics entering at Staircase, travelling over the First Divide and then on to Lake La Crosse where we left the trail, proceeded over Ranger Pass (Fisher's Notch) and then down to the Anderson Pass trail. We paused at Anderson Pass to climb Mt. Anderson and then went out the West Fork of the Dosewallips River.

The result of these activities was to put me in reasonably good shape for late August when George Martin invited me to join a party he was organizing to climb Mt. Olympus. His plan was to go in and out of the Hoh River so as to allow quick access to the summit, and to stay four days at a summit camp. I was anxious to go because I had never climbed Mt. Olympus, having been frustrated twice in the previous years by bad weather after long hikes into and out of the Queets Basin, so I quickly accepted his invitation.

A number of our regular climbing buddies who would normally have jumped at this opportunity were unable to do so because of other responsibilities so our group became a party of four, consisting of George Martin, Robert Scott, Don Dooley and myself. At this time, George Martin was vice principal of Bremerton High School, Bob Scott was a biology teacher at the same school and Don Dooley was a strong young high school student. In subsequent years Don was to establish quite a reputation as a mountaineer and climber, making a number of first ascents (see the chapter "Mt.Pershing" herein). George Martin, as many readers may know, later established the Outdoor Activities Program at Olympic Junior College, spending many years exploring and climbing in the Olympics and, most importantly, collecting and establishing a historical library of the area.

We arrived at the Hoh River trailhead about mid-afternoon after a long slow drive from Bremerton, so the late afternoon was spent hiking the 5 1/2 miles to Happy Four Shelter. This was my first trip up the Hoh River trail and I was deeply impressed by the beauty of what is so appropriatly called the Rain Forest. One should read Robert Wood's description of this trail in his Olympic Mountains Trail Guide to get a feel of this experience. Our second day was an uneventful hard trek with heavy packs up the remaining 12 miles to Glacier Meadows.

Day 3 took us into the high mountain country, but first I should describe how we were dressed and equipped for this "expedition". We all wore wool pants of various types along with a wool shirt or wool sweater. A light weight jacket suitable as a windbreaker and for light rain rounded out our attire. George Martin and Bob Scott had a two-man pup-tent no floor) into which four of us could crowd for a short period in an emergency (rain shower) but obviously if the weather turned bad we would be forced to retreat to the Glacier Meadows Shelter. We had one primus stove for all of us at our high camp. With respect to climbing gear, I was carrying 100 feet of 7/16" four-strand manilla rope plus an ice axe. I still do not understand why George Martin and Bob Scott were not carrying ice axes because they were using them the previous month on our Mt. St. Helens climb. Perhaps they had been rented or borrowed. Don Dooley tells me that he did not acquire one until the following year (1939). Of course during those depression years no one had much money and the cost of an ice axe represented a major purchase. As to boots, I was again the fortunate one, having had triconi nails and triconi edging nails installed by the Currin-Greene Boot Co. in Seattle in 1937. The others were using hob-nails. Since none of us was carrying crampons, boot nails became a significant factor on our early morning trip to Mt. Tom (described later). The 1930's crampons were heavy and rarely carried or needed in the Olympics, particularly if the climbers were equipped with triconis. I always felt comfortable in snow and ice with my triconi-nailed boots and ice axe.

Our party being thus equipped, I'm sure the reader will recognize that the success of our trip largely depended upon mild weather for soft snow.

Our start from Glacier Meadows on day 3 was in the clouds. Upon reaching the top of the moraine bordering the Blue Glacier we emerged from the clouds to a clear sky and bright sun. After an easy crossing of the Blue Glacier we started up to the top of the Snow Dome. It was probably at the first rest stop that I stripped to the waist—it was hot work but a fantastic sight. Below us was a sea of clouds and above blue sky and sun; a most auspicious introduction to the high country and I felt great as did, I am sure, my climbing companions. We proceeded up the soft snow to the top of the Snow Dome, then turned and headed for the West Peak ridge.

We passed through crevasse gulch to the left of 5-finger ridge, then scrambled up the short rock pitch to the top of 5-fingers where a beautiful flat campsite appeared. We dropped our packs (I don't remember where we ate lunch) and headed for West Peak, descending into the notch between 5-fingers and West Peak and then scrambling up to the summit. We were still above the sea of clouds with the many peaks of the Olympics massif projecting above the clouds. We could see the summit of Mt. Tom and the White Glacier, which defined the upper level of the cloud deck. George took his big camera out of his pack and began taking photographs. This was a large heavy camera that used 3 1/8" x 5 1/4" negatives in film packs similar to the "speed-graphic" but much more bulky than the popular 4" x 5" press style. It produced great pictures and the effort of getting it to many summits alone, with the skill of the photographer established George Martin as one of the greatest Olympic Mountain photographers.

My only other memory of the West Peak summit is that during our down-climb we encountered a fixed rope of some 80 feet to 100 feet hanging from the summit. My recollection is that it was about 3/4 " manilla and that we studiously avoided using it because it appeared to have been up there many years. I often wondered how long it had been in place and who had left it.

At camp on the top of 5-finger, George and Bob set up their tent and one of them added a flag on a short mast atop the tent. It was about 14 inches square and probably a bandana as it appears in an old photo. Recently I mentioned to Don Dooley that this flag must have a story behind it but neither of us could recall. It was probably a symbol that George was using to signify this as an "expedition" climb, not the ordinary in and out climb. After dinner and viewing a beautiful sunset through the cloud deck we "hit the sack" on the hard rocks. No such things as pads or air mattresses for our tired young bodies—we could sleep anywhere.

Day 4 dawned bright and clear, the low clouds from the previous day breaking up early. After a quick breakfast we set off across the upper Blue Glacier to do the remaining high peaks. As we approached Middle Peak Don had a big smile on his face and said to me "Maybe we'll have some good rock climbing here" but the smile disappeared when he saw that it was to be a simple class 3 scramble. Being an enthusiastic (and good) rock climber I think he was hoping for a class 5 experience. George indicated that he wanted to get atop East Peak early for photos, before the sun moved too far South, so we breezed past Middle Peak planning to climb it on our return.

Crossing the remaining distance to East Peak on the upper Blue Glacier was uneventful and we scrambled to East Peak's summit where George promptly set up his camera, taking photographs in all directions.

Since the day was young we agreed, after reviewing our options, that we should cross the upper Hoh Glacier and climb the highest unnamed peak to the south (later named Athena, or South Peak). From Athena we would go directly to Middle Peak on our return. After down-climbing East Peak we set off across the snowfield of the upper Hoh Glacier which became something of a slog in the softening snow. The rock climb up Athena was another scramble and George again set up his camera at the summit for a round of photos. Unlike the other three peaks to Olympus, we found no cairn or other evidence of earlier climbers.

After lunch on Athena our return to camp was via the upper Hoh Glacier to the summit of Middle Peak where George again did his photography, then back to 5-fingers camp. During dinner we made plans for the next day's trip to Mt. Tom. Don and I watched the sunset from our sleeping bags.

Day 5 again dawned bright and clear. After our usual breakfast we set out, descending the rock into Crevasse Gulch and then down the snowfield to the edge of the Snow Dome. I was carrying the rope and George had his camera and our lunch in his packsack. We turned west across the Snow Dome and descended to the top of the rock wall rising above the White Glacier. This rock was down-climbed until we reached a steep snowfield that extended to the White glacier. At the bottom of this snowfield there was a fairly large crevasse (I would judge eight to 10 feet wide) that extended approximately 2/3 of the width of the snowfield. The obvious route was to traverse across the top of the snowfield to clear the crevasse and from there to glissade on down to the glacier. The snow had set-up during the night and was too firm to easily kick steps so I set out chopping steps with my ice axe. I had taken perhaps half a dozen steps out on the traverse when I heard a shout and looking around saw Bob Scott on his back sliding feet first toward the crevasse, accelerating rapidly. Some years later, Don Dooley described it as follows:

"Bob Scott had just stepped across a moat to a steep snow slope. I was down-climbing the rock directly above him. As I briefly glanced up I saw him slip and then slide rapidly toward a crevasse. There was no way he could stop without an ice axe. I froze as I watched him shoot toward the upper lip of the crevasse. Within a few feet of the edge he surprisingly regained his feet in a standing glissade position.

Middle and West Peaks from East Peak.

West side of Blue Glacier. George Martin in foreground.

Olympus from Athena.

Mt. Tom from West Peak.

Athena from East Peak Olympus.

to say, there was a bit of good humored post-mortem talk as we walked toward Mt. Tom, such as "Where was your ice axe?," "What were you carrying the rope for?" etc. We certainly made a bundle of climbing errors.

From Mt. Tom a person has one of the most impressive views possible of the Olympus Massif and I particularly cherish the photo of that view taken by George. The return trip to camp was apparently no problem in the softer snow. All I recall was the long slog on the White Glacier.

Day 6 was our final and "going home" day. We got a very early start and traveled fast, reaching the trail head early enough to drive home that evening, ending one of the most remarkably successful climbs that I have ever made.

HENRY H. BOTTEN

When I returned to civilian life following WWII my first "boss" was a gentleman named Henry H. Botten, one of the foremost fire protection engineers in the country. As time went on we became good friends and I learned that he was an outdorsman, a woodsman, a hunter, had worked in lumber camps as a logger during summers while he was attending school, and that he and a few friends had built a hunting shack in the upper Elwha Basin. He was a close personal friend of Grant

Hume, accompanying Grant on many hunting and exploring trips in the Olympics.

When we got on the subject of mountain climbing, Henry said that he did not consider himself a climber but that he had climbed Mt. Rainier and also the three peaks of Olympus in 1908. When Henry learned that I had spent several days exploring the Olympus Massif in 1938, he warmed to the subject and described for me what he and his Bremerton friends had done in 1908, exactly thirty years earlier. From bits and pieces of subsequent conversations with Henry, and from The Mountaineers report on their First Annual Outing in 1907 I have pieced together the following story of the first traverse of the three Olympus summits in 1908.

In 1908 Henry Botten was employed at the Puget Sound Naval Shipyard in Bremerton, having recently been graduated from the University of Washington College of Engineering. His climbing partners on the 1908 Olympus traverse were George E. Hannaman, Alex Ormond, and William Spaulding who I understand were all residing in Bremerton at the time and probably also employed at the Puget Sound Naval Station. George Hannaman was a member of The Mountaineers and had been one of the leaders on their 1907 outing when The Mountaineers made many first ascents of peaks in the upper Elwha and Queets basins. They also climbed the West and Middle Peaks from the Queets Basin, so Hannaman was familiarwith these climbing routes. He was also probably the "spark plug" in organizing their 4-man 1908 trip. One can picture Hannaman's frustration at having been in the 1907 party that was forced back from Blizzard Pass because of a storm and his desire to return for another attempt. But he would have had little trouble in persuading his friends to join him on this attempt because according to Henry Botten all were eager to jump at any opportunity to explore new territory.

It was obviously a very strong fast-moving party. Henry Botten was a big, strong man, very confidant in himself both on and off the trail and I am sure Ormond and Spaulding were also experienced woodsmen. All knew how to take care of themselves. While, by modern day standards they had no climbing aids other than a rope, they all knew how to improvise when necessary. Henry always carried a long handled axe on the back of his pack and he knew how to use it. Experiences in logging camps taught him what hob nails and calks would do. Caulks (or corks) were preferred by loggers but his preference was hob nails. If Henry felt caulks would help on ice he would add a few to his hob nailed boots. Probably Hannaman was the only one carrying an alpine stock. Henry would cut a pole whenever he felt he might need one. Henry said that one or more members of any party always carried a rifle - they could live off the land if necessary. This was a turn of the century type exploring party.

With such a party, success was reasonably assured if they were favored with good weather. And they were so favored. Henry said that they decided since they were going so far in they might as well do the job right and climb all three peaks of Olympus, which is what they did. From a camp in Queets Basin they made the summits of West, Middle and East Peaks, returning to Queets Basin the same day. Henry remembered the climb as being uneventful except for seeing a lot of new and interesting country. As he had earlier told me, "I never really considered myself to be a mountain climber".

It was a privilege to have known Henry Botten and to have had the unique experience of following in his footsteps across the top of the Olympus massif and later these same footsteps throughout most of my professional career.

Henry, in the silent halls of memory, I salute you.

SECTION VI

The End of An Era

CHAPTER 21
CONSTANCE PASS

One of the most memorable days of my life occurred on June 1, 1942. It was the day I graduated from Washington State College (now WSU) with a Bachelor's degree in engineering. It was also the day that I became the owner of a brand new second lieutenant's commission in the U.S. Army Reserve.

Our whole class of reserve officers had been warned by the ROTC adviser at WSC that except for sudden death or the second coming of Christ we would all be on active duty in the army in less than 30 days, and not to go looking for permanent jobs because there was no deferment for us - ZERO. I don't believe any of us wanted out, anyway. Like nearly all other young men at the outbreak of World War II, we were anxious to serve, and as soon as possible.

My friend Swede Johnson, who had just completed his freshman year in forestry at WSC, suggested that inasmuch as I was one of the chosen few, why didn't I spend my few precious days with him? He had received a position as summer ranger on the Dosewallips River in the Olympic National Park and while he might put me to
work, it would be "fun". He had a radio and was in constant contact withe Park Service Headquarters at Port Angeles, so when I got my orders to active duty my parents could contact me through the National Park Service at Port Angeles.

It sounded good to me, so a few days after returning to Bremerton I asked my dad to drive me to Seabeck where I could catch a ferry to Brinnon. This he did that evening. After he dropped me off I walked aboard the ferry with my pack (no food included - I was on Swede's payroll) and was off to the Dosewallips River. After arriving in Brinnon I walked about two miles north along Hood Canal, then turned west up the Dose road, not knowing where Swede was, but determined to find him.

I had hiked only about half a mile when a pickup truck passed me, heading up river. It stopped, backed up, and the driver asked me if I wanted a ride. My answer, of course, was in the affirmative. There were three people in the front seat, so I threw my pack in the back of the truck and climbed in after it.

The three were members of the Civilian Conservation Corps (CCC) and were going 10 miles up the river to their camp, and that sounded great to me. When we arrived at the camp they very kindly asked me if I cared to stay for dinner, an invitation I couldn't refuse. They also offered a bunk and mattress for the night which I also accepted. The camp capacity was about 20 people, but a work party was absent, building trails farther up the river. There was a camp cook and two others and the seven of us spent the evening playing poker. They had very little money so were using matches for chips, and as I was also in the same fix this worked out well. Believe me, at the end of the evening I couldn't start a fire if I had a gallon of gasoline!

The conversation was all about closing down the camp because the national CCC program was being abolished as a result of the war. They had all been recruited into the CCC from Minnesota and Wisconsin, and had been told by their commanding officer (currently at a satellite camp further up the river) that the CCC program was ending at the end of the month. He said they would all be discharged and sent home. The boys all agreed they were going to take the trip home to see their families again, and then enlist in the service. They unanimously agreed they were going to make it the Navy. After the CCC experience the Army was out.

In the morning I had breakfast with them and asked if they knew Swede and his whereabouts. They all knew him and said that his headquarters was a tent on a platform about three miles on up at the end of the road. With this good news I left the CCC camp and headed in that direction. The ranger station was exactly as they described it, but there was no Swede. A sign pinned to the tent flap stated that the ranger was at Constance Pass, and all visitors were asked to sign the register in the adjacent weatherproof box, stating the date, name, number in party, destination and length of time expected before return.

I dutifully signed the register and started up river, on foot, for about three miles to the junction of the Constance Pass trail and the Dosewallips River trail. From there on the climb began. The trail to the pass was about five miles long and gained about 3,500 feet altitude in this distance. It was a good trail, but constantly climbing and placed a great strain on my out-of-shape body. A warm sunny day added to my discomfort. It was slow work and I was quite happy to see a tent just under the ridge above. As I slowly drew nearer I could make out Swede standing in front of the tent. I had covered 11 miles, it was mid-afternoon, and I was ready to quit for the day.

My comments about its being a rather strenuous trail caused him to smile and make the comment "A week ago I climbed up here with four car batteries on my pack. It weighed 108 pounds and was a helluva strain. It damn near broke the pack." That certainly shut me up. (Swede the year before had hiked from the trailhead on the Elwha River at Whiskey Bend over Hayden Pass and down to his tent ranger station, a distance of 46 miles and a vertical elevation change of 3/4 of a mile in one day - no camps).

He explained that the batteries were for the radio that he had inside the tent. This camp just below Constance pass had been established as part of the civil defense effort to watch for unidentified airplanes, and I understood that there were a number of these sites throughout the Olympics. He told me that this was not his job although he did oversee it and a couple of high school boys normally manned it. They were currently in Port Townsend for a three-day relief. Swede was just minding the store until they returned.

The tent wasn't very large, about seven feet by seven feet, and a person had to kneel inside. Two beds on the floor, the radio, a box supporting a Coleman camp stove and some groceries in a sheet metal food box filled it up. A small trickle of water nearby completed the facilities.

Swede griped about the civil defense kids' absence, as they were a day late in returning and Swede had more important things to do below. I, of course, had nothing better to do than stand in until their return so volunteered for the job. Swede was delighted, called up Port Angeles on the radio to explain the situation and get permission for the substitution. After explaining how the radio operated he left for the ranger station below, and I explored the food box to see what I would eat for dinner. There was a sack of rice and a small can of tuna fish that struck my fancy so I dined like an Oriental king - lots of rice.

The next morning Swede called from his radio at the station to ask facetiously if I'd seen any airplanes, then as an afterthought said "By the way, one of the airwatch guys is back and on the trail. You should see him this afternoon." As he had predicted, the boy arrived with a pack filled with groceries and a huge stack of pulp magazine westerns. We introduced ourselves; his name was Ralph, and I told him I'd get dinner. He said "fine-use this" and pulled three pounds of hamburger from the pack. It seemed strange eating food in a high mountain meadow you normally expect only in civilization. I guess I was subconsciously wishing it was macaroni and cheese. After dinner I admired the view and Ralph read pulps until dark when we went to bed.

When Swede and I had first discussed this trip to the Dosewallips while still at Washington State College, I had had an urge to explore Del Monte Ridge. This ridge runs almost due west of Constance Pass for a distance of about three miles, where it bumps into Mt. Mystery and terminates. Here I was, camped at one end of the ridge with a perfect opportunity to explore it. The next morning I headed up toward the ridge, but had traveled only a couple of hundred yards when I heard Ralph shouting and gesturing wildly. With trepidation I returned to camp, expecting to receive a call from Port Angeles.

Sure enough, Ralph, quite excited, said that Port Angeles had called and that I had received orders to active duty and must report at Benicia Arsenal, California on July 7, 1942. As this was already July 2nd, I had no time to lose. I started down the trail immediately, passing the second civil defense boy on the way, and getting to the ranger station in about three hours. Saying goodbye to Swede was difficult, as we both knew it would probably be a long time before we got together again. (See end of chapter 11.)

I left the ranger station and started hiking down the road to the highway and had walked about five miles when I was overtaken by a disgruntled fisherman in an old "woody" Chevy station wagon who stopped to give me a lift. He complained bitterly about his lack of success at catching fish in the famed Dose. Conversation disclosed that he was a fly fisherman from Bend, Oregon, and that he could do better than this and not even leave his home county.

As he told me he was returning to Seattle by ferry from Bremerton, I thought I would stick by this guy and ride all the way home with him. I suggested that he try the Staircase on the Skokomish River and extolled its fishing capabilities. That suited him, so we turned west at Hoodsport and were soon fishing.

He was fly fishing, having no luck and becoming quite bitter. I hadn't bought a fishing license that year, but asked if I could try it for a couple of casts. He agreed, so finding some of my favorite black beetles another ranger on the Dosewallips had introduced me to 20 years earlier, I superimposed one over the fly and made a couple of casts. Whango! I had a 12-inch Dolly racing all over the Skokomish River. I thought I'd quit right there, especially since I had no fishing license. I spent the rest of the afternoon chasing black beetles for him.

All good things come to an end, and we drove off away from the sunset toward Bremerton. The fisherman very kindly dropped me off on the south side of town, and after thanking him for the ride, stuck out my thumb on the road to Marine Drive. The third car passing was an acquaintance who took me right to my doorstep. It had been a long, busy day.

Two days later, I left Seattle on a Pullman, and 24 hours after that I became a soldier.

CHAPTER 22
GEORGE

George W. Martin became both my high school biology teacher and my Sunday school teacher more than 60 years ago. This beginning also launched an unforgettable partnership in hiking and climbing experiences. In the many years that I have been active in these activities I have met no one whose interest, enthusiasm and drive in pursuing them has been greater than that of George W. Martin. He did not claim to excel in any of them, although his achievements in these endeavors read differently. He was above all a great leader, with the ability to see desirable goals and then to recruit followers and pursue these goals to a satisfactory ending.

I first got to know George as a young boy as a member of Epworth League, a teenage group in the Methodist Church in Bremerton. My first impression of him was that of a large, tall man, over six feet, with a marvelous personality. He had been a college basketball player, and at that time he was the Bremerton High School basketball coach. He had a booming voice, always smiling, and I have never known him to be angry. George was a friend to everyone, a magnet for making strangers his friends and followers in interesting activities. He was married with two young daughters, and his devotion to his family showed in every aspect of his life.

Professionally, he was a school teacher and administrator. During my years in high school I remember him as a math and biology teacher, although his primary interest was in botany. His classes were very popular, and he spent many after school hours with students of similar interests. As early as 1936 he was organizing and leading members of the Epworth League on safaris to Mt. Rainier for a day of skiing or on nature hikes and picnics in the spring, summer and fall.

It was no surprise then that our small group of friends and former scouts invited him to join us in our mountain climbing and backpacking activities in the Olympic mountains. It didn't take long for him to become addicted. I believe this was a turning point in his life, as more and more of his time in the summers was involved in weekend climbs, although his church and school year activities still occupied his winters.

His mountain climbing, along with ours, became more and more advanced, and we made numerous ascents of the more prominent peaks in the Olympics. He faithfully carried his large and cumbersome camera with him (a 4x5 *Graflex*) together with additional film plates, everywhere he went in the mountains. The total weight must have been well over five pounds including film pack and tripod, and he accepted this added burden without complaint. He was a dedicated nature photographer all his life, and his black and whites were of superior quality, both in subject and artistic presentation.

Numerous climbs described herein cover some of these activities. Bob Scott, a close friend of George and another high school biology teacher also participated in a lot of our climbing activities, both during and after high school years, and these two acted as "governors" on our climbing ambitions. I am certain that without their adult judgement we would have had some very serious climbing problems.

As we grew older our life styles changed. Some of us went away to college, others married and moved to jobs in other communities, and with Pearl Harbor we were more or less permanently disbanded. I remember one summer, however, when I was home from school, that George and I and some college friends made a climb of Mt. Rainier. We bivouacked on Steamboat Prow on the north side of the mountain at about 10,000 feet elevation about three in the afternoon, and George was dragging a little. He stated that his stomach was a little upset. Shortly after midnight we prepared to continue up the mountain, and George indicated that he was much better. At about 11,500 feet he could not continue.

We had been marking the trail with wands so he decided he would follow the trail back to camp and wait for us. This was not acceptable to the rest of us and one of the others said he would accompany George to camp. George refused this until the volunteer stated he didn't think he could get to the summit anyway the way he was feeling. The two of them returned to camp and the rest of us were back in about eight hours.

Two more times George and I attempted Mt. Rainier, as he was determined to reach the summit. The third attempt was successful, for after a 24-hour acclimatizing rest at Steamboat Prow he was able to summit. After that he mentioned often that reaching the top of Mt. Rainier was one of the highlights of his life. His tenacity in climbing Mt. Rainier best describes one of the tenets of his life - a desire to do better. Although he subsequently made other successful ascents he always talked about our efforts.

Following World War II, I returned to Bremerton, but almost immediately moved to Bellevue as my new post-war job was in Seattle. Although visits to Bremerton were frequent, George and I traveled separate paths that never crossed, and shortly thereafter my family and I moved to Alaska. Unfortunately, I never was able to renew our friendship again. While most of my friends in our early hiking and climbing club, like me, had started new lives elsewhere, a few remained and their stories of George's later activities indicated that he had not slowed down.

After the conclusion of the war many new things came about in Bremerton, including the formation of Olympic College. This occurred in 1946, and its founders seized the opportunity to hire George Martin as the new college's registrar. His previous position in the Bremerton school system was that of vice principal at the Bremerton High School. The change provided new fields of leadership for him, including mountaineering.

George was still very much interested in hiking and climbing and continued his former outdoor pursuits with some of his old climbing buddies, primarily with Bob "Swede" Johnson. One of these climbs is described by Swede in the chapter herein entitled "The Needles".

An event that apparently had a major effect on his life occurred in 1951, when a 16 year-old boy took a bad fall on The Brothers, and although George and other experienced climbers were summoned and hastened to the accident site, they were too late. He felt strongly that this death might have been avoided.

In 1950, George was able to broaden his field of activities at

Olympic College and in addition to his full-time duties as registrar became active in initiating and promoting college courses in Basic Mountaineering and Wilderness Survival. The success of these courses prompted his addition of Campcraft.

The promotion and implementation of these courses had been an uphill battle, as approval at that time had to be obtained from the Kitsap County School Board and some of the Board members felt that the courses were not academically sound and were instead "recreations." It was in 1952, fortunately, that one of his greatest goals came to fruition and Olympic College came directly under the Administration of the State of Washington Dept. of Education. This office gave approval to Olympic College to offer credit courses in outdoor activities. As far as can be determined these were the first accredited courses of this kind in the nation. Many colleges and universities have since followed suit, in some instances using George's curriculum as a guide.

This one move did more for the advancement and safety of mountaineering, hiking and camping in the Pacific Northwest than any other single factor, for the college churned out thousands of students that had completed his outdoor courses and were prepared to avoid accidents, and to cope with those that did occur.

Memories of the boy's death on The Brothers in 1951 had a definite influence on the curriculum of George's mountaineering courses; he felt strongly that proper training might have avoided not only that death, but many others as well. These memories were still strong, so in 1957 he was one of the principal instigators in the formation of the Olympic Rescue Group.

Now, with the full backing of the Dept. of Education, George was able to broaden his outdoor courses. He expanded them to include two 15-day summer hikes into the Olympics each summer with as many as 30 students attending each course. These classes were mobile during the 15-day period, provisioned by pack horses, and usually started at Solduc Hot Springs. The class hiked in, camping at Deer Lake and Hoh Lake en route, with a base camp usually established somewhere near Glacier Meadows.

While encamped at Glacier Meadows all students who were

interested were offered a summit climb of 7,965 foot Mt. Olympus, highest point in the range. Accompanying faculty provided daily lectures,with Botany and Zoology instructor Robert Scott, Geology by

George W. Martin.

Ruth Baldwin, and meteorology by John Mandeck. Additional leaders were included to provide essential camping, hiking and climbing skills. Other summer classes, with similar goals, were similarly offered for family groups, including small children, although the itinerary was somewhat reduced, and hiking and camping skills were stressed.

George was the driver for all of these summer outdoor classes for a period of 12 years, from 1952 to 1964, when he retired. At that time he turned the leadership over to Dave Sicks, his able assistant, who continued the classes until 1974 when they were no longer offered. This was brought about by two factors. The National Park Service had placed a restriction on the size of sanctioned parties entering the Olympic National Park, and the action of the college president at that time who did not want the program to continue.

After retirement he was as busy as ever, traveling around the world hiking, climbing, visiting other countries, or writing articles, giving lectures, serving on conservation and recreation group committees; basically carrying on his lifetime of activities. He never stopped preaching the wilderness ethic from 1930 when he became involved in the things he loved - the meadows, peaks, glaciers and rivers of the Olympic Mountains - until his death in 1970.

He was, in fact, delivering a nature lecture on the evening of September 1st when he suffered a coronary. On September 8th he passed away. His lifetime was a continuous, fulfilling love affair with the Olympic Mountains that continued to its end. He was one of the fortunate few.

George W. Martin was born June 24,1901 in Kansas, attended schools in Douglas County and Spokane and graduated from the University of Washington in 1930 with degrees in Math and Biology, later receiving a Master's Degree in Botany.

It has been an honor and a great privilege to have been included as one of his earlier hiking and climbing partners. I will be forever grateful that we were able to explore the Olympics, learning and enjoying new mountain experiences together. His passing has left a hollow spot in many lives.